"What a story! A courageously transparent father and son honest of their weaknesses so that God is clearly the hero in this life-and-death struggle of addiction and religion versus relationship—on so many levels! Every parent should get this as a handbook because it clearly illustrates the long, hard journey of parenting any child. It helped me trade my shame and guilt for a thirst for fervent prayer and unconditional-love relationships with my kids and grandkids for the long, long haul. The title sums it up well, hope does lie ahead!"

ROBBY DILMORE, nationally syndicated radio show host

"There is one particular line in the children's fable *The Velveteen Rabbit* that always moves me to tears: 'You are a terribly real thing in a terribly false world, and that, I believe, is why you are in so much pain.' Reading James and Geoff's story instantly reminded me of that line. *Hope Lies Ahead* is a must-read for any family pulled at the seams by addiction, rebellion, or pain. It is a painfully beautiful tapestry of the heart of a father, the desperation of a prodigal, and the hope found in Jesus. More than anything, James and Geoff's willingness to wrestle with vulnerability is a living corroboration that love really does never fail."

STUART HALL, director of Student Leadership and Leadership Networking for Orange (ReThink Group); leader of INFLUNSR; speaker, author, and coach

"Triumph out of tragedy. It is not just a pie-in-the-sky slogan but a testament to the redeeming grace of God. Never is this truth more beautiful than in our families. In recent years, I've been blessed to pray with my friend James Banks as we have watched triumphant grace bring miracles in his son's life. Now, through the pages of *Hope Lies Ahead*, we can all trace God's redemption in this raw but real account of Geoff's journey of transformation and subsequent call to fruitful ministry. If you have a prodigal or know anyone who does, make this your next book because God has tailor-made doses of hope and healing for all.

DANIEL HENDERSON, president and founder of Strategic Renewal International; author of *Transforming Prayer: How Everything Changes When You Seek God's Face*

HOPE

lies ahead

Encouragement for Parents of Prodigals
from a Family That's Been There

James Banks & Geoffrey Banks

Our Daily Bread
Publishing™

Requests for permission to quote from this book should be directed to: Permissions Department, Our Daily Bread Publishing, PO Box 3566, Grand Rapids, MI 49501, or contact us by email at permissionsdept@odb.org.

Interior design by Sam Carbaugh.

Library of Congress Cataloging-in-Publication Data

Names: Banks, James, 1961- author. | Banks, Geoffrey, author.
Title: Hope lies ahead : encouragement for parents of prodigals from a
    family that's been there / James Banks & Geoffrey Banks.
Description: Grand Rapids, MI : Our Daily Bread Publishing, 2020. |
    Includes bibliographical references. | Summary: "James Banks and his son
    Geoff Banks each write from their perspective of Geoff's prodigal
    journey. You'll find encouragement to pray deeply, love generously, and
    cling to God for comfort, healing, and restoration during the difficult
    journey"-- Provided by publisher.
Identifiers: LCCN 2019046779 (print) | LCCN 2019046780 (ebook) | ISBN
    9781640700055 (paperback) | ISBN 9781640700604 (ebook)
Subjects: LCSH: Parent and child--Religious aspects--Christianity. |
    Parents of problem children--Religious life.
Classification: LCC BV4529 .B355 2020 (print) | LCC BV4529 (ebook) | DDC
    248.8/45--dc23
LC record available at https://lccn.loc.gov/2019046779
LC ebook record available at https://lccn.loc.gov/2019046780

Printed in the United States of America
20 21 22 23 24 25 26 27 / 8 7 6 5 4 3 2 1

*Dedicated to all who have ever prayed for a prodigal—
and especially to those who prayed for our own.*
JAMES

*Dedicated to those who are still battling in their
addiction and to their families who love them.*
GEOFF

CONTENTS

Introduction 9

1. Breath of Life 13

2. Of Prodigal Paths and Clenched Fists 21

3. "You Don't Get a Casserole" 31

4. "Today Was a Good Day" 44

5. A Far Country 58

6. Squandered near Angels 69

7. A Tougher Love 82

8. In the Shadow 95

9. "Jesus Camp" 110

10. New Creation 124

11. Power and Authority 135

12. Overtaken by Love 146

Acknowledgments 159
Appendix A: *Excerpts from* Prayers for Prodigals   162
Appendix B: Resources 167
Notes 169

INTRODUCTION

The end of a matter is better than its beginning,
and patience is better than pride.
—ECCLESIASTES 7:8

The fact that my son Geoff and I can write this book together is nothing less than a miracle. We've been on a long and difficult journey together, and it's only because of God's mercy and kindness that we are able to tell about it.

Imagine for a moment that you could sit down with the father in the parable of the prodigal son years after the son came home (Luke 15:11–32) and talk with him about all that had happened during that challenging time. What was he going through at home when his son was in the far country? How did he get through the day when someone he loved deeply was in such a bad way? What was it that made him run to his son when the young man was still "a long way off" (Luke 15:20), instead of turning his back and disowning him? Then imagine that while you're having that conversation his son is also in the room, filling in the details from his own perspective. His son isn't the prodigal he once was, but he knows how prodigals think. He's been there. He's learned from his mistakes (the hard way). Both his glance and his words are direct.

That conversation is what you have in this book. In each chapter, I will begin with my perspective, and Geoff will follow up with his. Ours is a story about much more than addiction. It is about sins and mistakes we both made and the love that met us nonetheless. It is about the power of prayer (a lot of prayer!) and forgiveness and learning how to cling to God in the dark. It's also about the new beginnings He alone can give.

Just like in the parable of the prodigal, there's celebration in this book. My son "was lost and has been found" (Luke 15:24 NASB), so you'll find some joy in these pages and also some shouts and sighs of relief. There might even be dancing. But just remember this: when dads dance, even though it may be old-school and out of fashion, it's still from the heart.

We would like to ask you just one favor as you read this book. Please don't be "an older brother." You know the guy. "The older brother became angry and refused to go in" to the party (Luke 15:28). He had his reasons. He knew what his younger brother had done, and he held it against him. Because we have tried to be as open and honest as possible, there will be places where it would be easy to judge us. But please read our story gently. Part of our motivation in sharing our past—faults and all—is that we want to encourage others to take the same risk. Our churches need to be places where people can be honest about their struggles, so we can pray for each other and love each other into the help that God alone can give.

It's all about getting to Jesus. Just think about some of the people Jesus hung out with. Do you remember what the uptight religious folks said about Him in the very same chapter of Luke, right before He gave us the parable of the prodigal? "This man welcomes sinners and eats with them" (Luke 15:2). Yes, He does, and that's something to celebrate!

In the end, the parable of the prodigal son isn't about an earthly father at all. It's about love incarnate who came to save us all. As I wrote in my book *Prayers for Prodigals*, "Jesus is God seeing us in the distance and looking on us with compassion. He is God running to us and throwing His arms around us. He is heaven's kiss welcoming the repenting sinner home."[1]

He is all of those things and more—infinitely more! It is our prayer (mine and Geoff's) that you will meet Him here. His fingerprints are traceable on every page of our story. "To him be the glory forever!" (Romans 11:36).

JAMES BANKS

1

BREATH OF LIFE

JAMES

*The extreme greatness of Christianity lies in the
fact that it does not seek a supernatural remedy
for suffering, but a supernatural use for it.*
SIMONE WEIL, *GRAVITY AND GRACE*

Geoff was almost born in the car.

It was a sunny summer morning, and I was scheduled to preach
sixteen miles away at a church in Ojai, California. Cari's labor
started early that morning, but after a quick checkup our doctor
assured us that Cari and the baby were healthy, and there was
enough time for me to make the trip. So she stayed at home and
rested while her mother took care of her.

After the service I had the distinct feeling I shouldn't stick around to shake hands. I headed back (a little faster than I should have) over the winding mountain road between Ojai and Santa Paula with the top down on my 1964 Plymouth Valiant convertible. Yet when I arrived home, Cari insisted that we wait longer.

Cari wanted our son to be born as naturally as possible. She had taken great care of herself throughout both of her pregnancies, but our daughter (born eighteen months earlier) was delivered via C-section due to a frank breach presentation at birth. Our doctor informed us that Cari would likely be able to have a natural delivery this time, but because of the previous C-section it was considered a somewhat higher risk. Still, Cari's goal was to spend as little time at the hospital as possible.

Soon the contractions began coming so quickly that we knew we had to leave. On the quick road trip to the hospital, we drove past our friend Carol's house, the top still down on the car. She told us later, "I saw you guys and knew what was happening. I had to laugh. Cari, you looked fine. James, you were white as a sheet."

Eleven minutes after we arrived at the hospital, Geoffrey was born. There wasn't even time to put in an IV. Our doctor, who was also working the emergency room that day, met us at the door and led us to a birthing room. But as Geoff began to emerge, something unexpected occurred. The umbilical cord was caught around his neck, and his breathing was compromised. Dr. Tubbs examined the cord and moved his hands quickly in the air, calculating the direction the cord was wrapped and rehearsing his next move. Moments later he skillfully removed the loop.

Suddenly Geoffrey was there, with broad little shoulders and a head full of dark brown hair. But he had yet to draw breath, and his little face was darkening quickly. Dr. Tubbs checked his air passages while we waited. Seconds passed like hours.

Then it came—a hesitant sound crescendoing into a full-throated, deep-chested cry. Geoffrey took his first breath, and we breathed deeply and wept. Our hearts were full as we held our beautiful boy in our arms and welcomed God's gift of life with wide-eyed wonder.

Like rapids on a river that come out in a calm place, the dramatic moments at Geoff's birth would be behind us for a time. Little did we know that those first rough water moments of waiting and worry were only a precursor of difficult moments to follow. Those would occur years later—but at that time we were happily anticipating every day to come. My close friend John visited us in the hospital room that afternoon. As he held Geoffrey in his arms, he looked at him thoughtfully and then looked at us: "Have you given this baby to God?" he asked. We bowed our heads together in that moment, praying that Geoffrey would one day know Jesus as his Savior and walk with God into a full and blessed life.

Geoffrey's childhood was blessed. His early years were idyllic. He was happy and loved—and lovable. He was surrounded by people who cared for him, and every physical and emotional need was met. His life was filled with fun and friends and sports and faith. We read to him daily, and he was there with us in church and Sunday school week after week, year after year.

Never in our worst nightmares would we have thought that this winsome, bright little guy would one day be a prodigal. Yet that is indeed what happened. When we think back over our son's life, we realize that one of the hardest things about being the parent of a prodigal is the nagging thought that I should have done something differently. Even though our children make their own choices—possibly choices that we ourselves never would have made at their age, still we wonder, *Couldn't I have changed the circumstances under which those choices happened?* We replay the past in our heads and look at that friend, or that school, or any other number of contributing factors and think, *If I had only known, we never would have gone there.*

But that's where the problem lies. Even though you do your best to be there for your child and to be attentive, there's so much that escapes us. There is a sense of guilt, as if we should have known.

Twenty-twenty hindsight glares at us judgmentally from our past, even though there was no way of knowing what would happen at the time. How could we know—how could we have control over every circumstance, every decision our children make? And how could we know that decisions that seemed good at the time would have such devastating consequences?

We can feel this even more deeply when we see families around us who seem to have it all together. Just as it's always easier to tell someone how they should raise their kids (parents of prodigals are sometimes the recipients of that kind of advice), it's also easy to slip into thinking that others' lives with their children are painless and trouble free. The child who is getting straight As and high honors doesn't struggle in the same way as the one who is getting drunk or high. But both may be just as far from God. Parents who have done what they can to lovingly share their faith at home will feel that weight.

Parents of prodigals often struggle in silence. It's easy to feel that when we come to church we can't share what is really going on at home, and it's not just because we're worried about what others will think. It's just that the problems are complicated, and they take time to share. And we may have brought our problems to God so many times that we feel prayed out and have run out of words. Still, God's Word affirms that He cares so deeply that He tracks every tear: "You keep track of all my sorrows. You have collected all my tears in your bottle" (Psalm 56:8 NLT).

An old hymn affirms, "No one understands like Jesus." We see this clearly in an incident recounted by John when Jesus encounters a man who was blind from birth. His disciples ask, "Rabbi, who sinned, this man or his parents, that he was born blind?" (John 9:2). That question hits too close to home for the parents of prodigals. If we're honest with ourselves, we see vestiges of our own depravity in our children and shake our heads at the mess. But Jesus wouldn't go there. "Neither," he responded. "This happened so that the works of God might be displayed in him" (v. 3).

That's a great spiritual starting point for those who are wondering what to do next as they walk through prodigal years. Jesus doesn't look backward; he looks ahead. When it's easy to look for someone to blame, Jesus doesn't do it. And when he does talk about the past, there's nothing bitter about it. Just a reference to something that God can redeem.

Hope lies ahead. And that is because the Good Shepherd whose "goodness and love will follow" us "all the days" of our lives (Psalm 23:6) overtakes us in unexpected places. God's redeeming love is so indefatigable that He is able to take something the enemy has twisted and bend it back to a blessing. Roads that we wish we had never gone down can come out in places that are breathtakingly beautiful, precisely because of where we have been—and we could not have gotten there any other way.

"This happened so that the works of God might be displayed in him." Little did we know—when our prayers seemed to go unanswered or when we sat in the courtroom and wept or when we visited rehab for the umpteenth time—that God would use Geoff's story to bring hope and encouragement to parents and prodigals all over the world.

We'll share our story here as candidly as we can—Geoff in his own words and I in mine. But the last word is God's. He brings light out of darkness and makes hope shine forth just when it seems like none can be found. "Now to him who is able to do immeasurably more than all we ask or imagine, according to his power that is at work within us, to him be glory in the church and in Christ Jesus throughout all generations, for ever and ever! Amen" (Ephesians 3:20–21).

GEOFF

I woke up cold, angry, and sick. It was about four in the morning, and I was lying on a hard, cement, jail-cell floor on an inch-thick mat. Because of rampant drug addiction in our area, the county lockup was overpopulated, and there were no bunks left to sleep on. Being a heroin addict, I couldn't go more than six hours without dosing or I would be horribly sick. It had been almost twenty-four. Every inch of my body was in pain, and my skin was crawling.

I couldn't think straight or even form coherent sentences, but one thing continually ran through my head: *How did I end up here? How did I end up like this?* When I started using drugs, I never even thought about where it would take me. I didn't want to be an addict. Nobody ever does. We just want to feel alive.

A week prior to waking up on that floor, I was desperate. I had a hefty heroin addiction, and I couldn't hold down a job longer than a week. This led to all sorts of nefarious methods of getting money: selling drugs, robbing people, or stealing from my family. I did whatever it took to feel okay. To feel normal. It never seemed as though I was doing something wrong; I thought I had to do these things to survive. That feeling is almost indescribable. It's an instinctual need deep down in your stomach that gnaws at your soul until you satisfy it.

Earlier that day, I had driven over to a friend's house, but I'm not sure what exactly was on my mind. If he was home, I was just going to hang out. But if he wasn't, I knew what I was there for. I knocked on the door to no avail and went around to the back to see if he was asleep on the couch. His sliding glass door was unlocked, so I let myself in. After walking around my friend's home and calling out for him, I realized no one was home.

A normal person would have left, but I wasn't that kind of person. I immediately began scanning the room for something of value—something that would help me feel normal. My eyes finally rested on a large rifle that was hanging on the wall of the hallway. Without thinking, I wrapped it in a blanket, left the house, and tossed it in the back of the car—already anticipating the drugs this would score me.

I didn't realize—or perhaps I didn't care—that stealing that gun would lead to my arrest and a nightmarish detox on the floor of an overpopulated jail. I thought it was a quick fix to all my problems.

When I look back at those years of my life, that seemed to be my mantra. I didn't realize I would end up in jail. I didn't realize I would be addicted. I didn't realize I would hurt my family. I didn't realize my friends would die. I didn't realize this wouldn't fulfill me. I didn't realize how lost I was.

In the beginning, my life didn't seem like it was careening toward addiction and crime. I had a storybook childhood, better than most of the kids around me. I grew up in an awesome neighborhood with lots of friends, and I made great grades. Doing school and making friends seemed easy to me. Teachers and parents alike told me how intelligent I was and how good looking I was, and they encouraged me with phrases such as "If you put your mind to it, you can do anything you want."

It's easy to look at an ideal situation like mine and wonder why I would do what I did—why I would take the gifts God gave me and exchange them for drugs and crime. How could I make such a decision? Did I want to hurt the people I loved, or did I not just care?

The truth is, I never wanted to hurt anyone or disappoint a soul, but somehow I did exactly that. Addicts desperately want to please people; they desperately try to make people happy. With misinformed intentions and a deceived mind, I quickly followed pleasure toward the grave.

Somewhere in my life I had become dependent on compliments. When I heard someone affirm me, it temporarily filled my massive need for acceptance—this God-given demand for love. Little did I know that no human love could ever satiate that need. As time went on, I tried time and time again to fill it. When I moved from grade school to middle school, my social importance moved from my family and teachers to my friends and peers. Instead of wanting to hear "You did a great job, son," I settled for "Dude, that was so cool!" I slowly got sucked into a bad crowd, and the downward spiral began.

In reality, we all have this same need for love, and we all spend time trying to fill it with deficient things. Some of us attempt with success or a relationship, while others try with drugs. There is a myriad of false satisfactions in the world, and often we don't understand when someone chases after an unfamiliar one. Moreover, we often don't see how we do the same thing in a different way—running from God in pursuit of ourselves. So we carry on looking at others, becoming frustrated and sometimes giving up. We don't realize that the battle is too difficult to tackle alone, for "we do not wrestle against flesh and blood, but against the rulers, against the authorities, against the cosmic powers over this present darkness, against the spiritual forces of evil in the heavenly places" (Ephesians 6:12 ESV).

It was a battle I was not prepared for, so it took me from the comfort of a loving Christian family to the unbearably uncomfortable floor of a county jail. I was one of the sick, the unbelieving, and the addicted that Jesus came to save. But I wanted no part of what He had to offer.

2

Of Prodigal Paths and Clenched Fists

James

A proud man is always looking down on things and people; and of course, as long as you are looking down, you cannot see something that is above you.
—C. S. Lewis, *Mere Christianity*

"That's my boy!"

Sure, it's a well-worn phrase. But every dad who's had a son wants to say it. Those words describe that fulfilling moment when you catch your son in the act of achieving something really good—and you proudly see him as an extension of yourself.

"That's my boy!" "That's my girl!"

Funny how we use those words to describe only the best moments. Our children are just as much our own when they're doing things we're not proud of, but we naturally want them to reflect those things that represent the best in us.

That's not all bad. When we revel in our children and call them our "pride and joy," we show something of our Father's heart, who "saw all that he had made, and it was very good" (Genesis 1:31). There's no sin in a warm-hearted admiration or grateful appreciation for something or someone outside of ourselves.[2]

The problem comes when we cling too tightly and take credit for too much. Sometimes we become so enamored with the gift that we take our eyes off the Giver. When we find ourselves thanking God less for the blessings in our lives and imagining we somehow deserve them, we are grasping for glory where we shouldn't. If we're not careful, we can hang on to what we love so tightly that we find ourselves standing before God with clenched fists once it begins to slip away.

I remember the "glory days" with Geoff. He was in middle school and had just been promoted to captain of the lacrosse team. He loved lacrosse and was good at it. The team had new uniforms—blazing orange and black—and Geoff was a picture of health as he ran up and down the field and made plays. I watched him play late one afternoon as the warm southern sun seemed to paint all that it touched with a golden hue.

The field was golden. Geoff was golden. Life was golden. *It doesn't get any better than this*, I thought. I stood on the sidelines and basked in the moment.

Those were good days, and I had every reason to believe they would continue.

But they ended abruptly with a phone call one afternoon: "Mr. Banks, your son has been arrested for possession of a controlled substance."

WHAT??? Something inside of me shouted in disbelief. But I didn't say a word.

The voice on the other end continued officiously: "He's being charged with distribution. You need to come to the school immediately."

"There's got to be some kind of a mistake," I reasoned. "I'll be there right away."

But there was no mistake. Geoff had been caught with a plastic bag containing several prescription meds. Another student had seen him with them and turned him in. There were enough pills in the bag for him to be charged with selling them.

We sat in the principal's office together.

"They weren't for me, Dad," Geoffrey insisted, "and I wasn't selling them. They were for a friend. Someone gave them to me to give to him."

I wanted to believe him. But he had been clearly caught with them, and there were far too many questions.

"Why would you do that?" was the best I could muster out of my shock and dismay. I began to wonder about what I didn't know and how long I didn't know it.

"What friend were they for and what friend were they from?" I queried.

"I'm not going to rat him out," Geoff answered. He said nothing more, silently staring at the wall.

There was hurt in his eyes. I could see it. But he wouldn't let me in to understand the cause of it. Suddenly there was a whole part of his world I no longer had access to. I wanted so much to reason with him and to help him, but I had been locked out.

"This is bad, Geoff."

More silence.

This time the principal intervened: "Because he's a minor he'll be released to your custody. But he will be suspended from school, and he will have to go to court. I suggest you get an attorney."

The meeting took mere minutes but seemed to last forever. And the ride home, while just a few miles, seemed even longer.

"How could you do this?" I asked angrily once we were alone in the car. "You're going to have a criminal record now."

No answer.

"Do you know what other people are going to think about our family when this gets out?"

"It's not about you, Dad."

He had a point, but I couldn't see it. I had grown up in a small town where my dad had been a college professor and mayor, and now I was a pastor—so I felt that others were always watching. Dad, a decorated combat veteran of two wars, had inculcated in me a strong sense of respect and family identity, which (for my part) was probably closer to pride than I cared to admit. It wasn't that way for Dad—he was simply from a generation that thought your word was your bond and your name should mean something. If you didn't own much but still had integrity and a good name, you had the world.

Now it seemed like our world was crumbling at the edges. No one in my family had ever done anything like this that I knew of. I had never seen the inside of a courtroom in my life. These were uncharted waters for me, like the old illuminated maps where beyond the known expanse of the sea there were illustrations and the words "Here be dragons." The dragon of drugs had extended an ugly claw into my son, and there was little I could do to stop it.

In the weeks that followed, we grounded Geoff. Cari and I made sure he stayed current on his school homework during the suspension period. We did our best to reason with him and tried to carefully screen who he had contact with. We searched his room and his backpack for any signs of substance abuse and tried to stay actively engaged in his life. We also found ourselves praying more—alone and as a couple.

There was progress. We saw some softening in Geoff, indications that he realized at least a little of the gravity of what he had done and was remorseful. But we never found out where the pills came from, and that was frustrating.

Allegiances were shifting in Geoff's mind and heart. Where once we had been his world, now we found ourselves on the outside knocking, asking to be let in.

Cari handled it better than I did. She had ways of gently loving Geoff and affirming the good in him in little, daily things. But I was angry—and even though "human anger does not produce the righteousness that God desires" (James 1:20), somehow I felt justified in it. I wanted to kick in the door of the distance between us and set things right.

I felt my son slipping away, and I thought I had to do something. Where was the little boy I had been so close to, that boy who was so sweet and open? When did he gain this interest in pills, and how long had we not known? What if he hurt himself—or worse? How could we turn him from this, and what kind of a future did he have if we couldn't? Who had led him on this path, and why had he gone down it? What kind of friends did he have who thought this was okay?

There were so many questions. And at times I found myself forcefully interrogating Geoff—which just caused the distance to increase. One conversation in particular took a hard turn:

"You're better than this, Geoff."

"No, I'm not, Dad."

"Do you know what kind of people do this sort of thing? Losers!" I emphasized the word to give it weight. "You're not a loser, are you?"

Geoff's eyes met mine angrily for a moment, then he looked at the floor.

I wanted my words to hurt, thinking they might somehow jar him back into reason. But I didn't realize how unreasonable I was being.

My words betrayed a way of looking at the world that was very different from Jesus's way. Instead of seeing others as broken sinners (like me), people in need of a Savior who loved them, I had divided the world into groups of winners and losers—making it clear which side I felt I was on. Anger and pride—pride that stems from self-focus and concern over what others think—made clear that my heart had a lot of room to grow in love.

Instead of still saying, "That's my boy" to a child who had erred and strayed, identifying with him in his weakness so I could point him to the way out, I had allowed "That's my boy" to be bitterly twisted and turned into an attitude of "That's not my boy."

And that was just making things worse.

GEOFF

Look at me, I'm a loser, I'm a winner, I'm good, I'm bad. I'm a sinner, I'm a killer. What I'm doing, I'm saying that I'm human.
KENDRICK LAMAR, "KUSH AND CORINTHIANS (HIS PAIN)"

I can remember a time as a child when everything my parents did was gold. They were the most intelligent people in the world, and I wanted nothing more than to impress them and do things that would make them proud. But as time rolled on, I grew up. My eyes began to shift from my parents to the world around me. I stopped looking to Mom or Dad for an example and began to look elsewhere. As I began to look around, I found so many people I thought worthy of imitation.

Growing up in a culture where people around me championed gang members and drug dealers, I slowly learned to do the same. I thought, *Here are some people who have it all.* So my interests began to change. And so did I.

How do we become the person we are? It is a complicated question to ask. I once heard a popular pastor quip, "We would have to know the entire history of the universe and everything that had ever come to pass to truly understand how anything came to be in its current state." There are so many different factors that shape our identity and our personalities, and the age-old question of nature or nurture stands unanswered in the face of so many variables.

As human beings we tend to find people we want to be like, and we attempt to mirror them as best we can. We carry this habit with a certain level of diffidence, and we often deny the truth of it by saying things like "I don't care what people think about me" or "I just want to be my own person." But these common proverbs couldn't be further from the truth.

While I had been taught by my family and my church that I was created in God's image and that I was supposed to imitate Jesus, I pushed in the other direction, finding friends and cultural icons to look up to and try to be like.

As I chased after my new identity, being fooled into thinking I was someone original, I began to change. I traded my dreams of playing sports and succeeding academically for facades of street smarts, quick money, and being feared and respected.

I remember my first taste of this in middle school. I had chased after this image of being a street kid so much that I would lie to people to attempt to create a reality that I didn't really live in. Friends would ask me things like, "You ever smoked weed before?" and I would quickly answer affirmatively—knowing that eventually the opportunity would present itself.

One day it finally did.

A group of friends asked me if I wanted to skip class and go smoke at a kid's house—a guy who didn't live far from my school. So there I went, walking out of the middle school with a high school girl who pretended to be my aunt so she could sign me out of class. This was it! This was the reality I was looking for. Here was my opportunity to cultivate the image of being a rebel.

That day I did drugs for the very first time. I inhaled deeply and waited for some sort of bliss to overtake me. I didn't know what to expect, but as soon as it hit me, I knew I loved it. I knew I didn't want to stop. I immediately began to think, *If weed can make me feel like this, what can all those other drugs do?* This experience started a fascination with drugs and the way they affected me. I would never be the same again.

Later that day, I got dropped back off at school during my last period. There was some sort of school event happening that day because I remember walking up to my group of friends out on the football field and feeling like the king of the world.

I did it! I was beginning to become the person I so badly wanted to be. I boasted about how I had been hanging out with high school kids all day long and that I was high as a kite. My friends thought I was the coolest person in the world.

That was it. That feeling. That rush.

Hearing the kids in the hallway whisper about what you did and what a rebel you were! That was what I was looking for all along. Or so I thought. So I kept walking that path and waiting for opportunities to prove myself. Slowly but surely, I began to progress further into a life I thought was perfect for me.

I was in eighth grade that year and had been dating a girl since the beginning of school. Her mom had undergone surgery, so she had a substantial amount of opiates lying around the house.

This was the beginning of the OxyContin craze in the 2000s, and no one thought to lock up their prescription meds. It was unthinkable that a middle schooler would take them to get high, but that is exactly what we did. After gaining an affinity for these tiny white pills, I decided to pocket some to take to school the next day. It is strange how something so small can captivate our hearts and minds so strongly.

I walked into school the next day unaware that I would be leaving under much different circumstances. When the sheriff came to my class and asked me to step outside, I had two conflicting feelings. First, I was scared, knowing something bad was going to happen. The pills in my pocket felt like they were on fire.

But there was something else. I was exhilarated: A sheriff came to my class to pull me out! This was just adding to my image. I had some perverted sense of pride about the whole school knowing I was in trouble.

It wasn't until I was in front of the principal and my father that the reality of the situation hit me. This image I had cultivated was supposed to be for my friends and the people at school. My dad wasn't supposed to be in on this.

I was someone else at home; I was actually a good kid. I still made good grades, I still played lacrosse and fenced, I was still making my parents proud. Now my false front was broken. They knew. Everyone knew.

In a strange way, my secret identity being revealed to my parents was actually a relief. I didn't have to hide anymore. They knew the truth. I had exhausted myself trying to cover up any clue they could find that would point to my lifestyle at school. Now I would no longer find myself trying to hide it as much from anyone. People knew, and I didn't care.

Maybe I would have cared if the people who knew had approached me out of pity, or if they would have come to me feeling bad for the mistakes I was making out of ignorance. However, this was never the response. When people who were a part of my normal life began to find out I was using drugs, the response was frequently visceral. Anger and shock abounded, which led to pain on my part.

Because I was so hurt I could think of nothing else to do but lash out. I returned their anger with spite and did things in an attempt to get revenge. The pain I felt drove me deeper into the world I was just beginning to scratch the surface of.

I felt as though society was beginning to reject me. Teachers, church members, and coaches loved me when I did what they wanted me to do. Make good grades, be kind to people, follow the rules, read my Bible. When I followed the playbook, I was accepted and loved. But when I went off script and began to make mistakes that people never would've expected, their perception of me changed.

As I wandered closer to the outskirts of my social circle, I slowly lost the acceptance and admiration I once lived for. I didn't want to be secretive, but I also didn't want to be alone. So I began to gravitate toward a new community. It was a community that would accept me for who I thought I was and encourage the lifestyle I wanted to live.

As the people I surrounded myself with changed, so did the places I wanted to be. I used to love going to church on Sunday to see people and hang out with a few friends I had, but I began to grow uncomfortable walking in the doors. I did whatever I could to avoid going.

I also slowly phased hobbies out of my life. Experimenting with drugs had become the only hobby I wanted. I stopped skating, playing lacrosse, and fencing. With everything I was putting my body through, I couldn't keep up anyway. My soul had begun to shrink to the size of my greatest concern: using drugs.

3

"You Don't Get a Casserole"

James

I'm not young enough to know everything.
J. M. Barrie, *The Admirable Crichton*

"We need to have a reunion at your house," Robert sighed wistfully.

Robert was one of Geoff's neighborhood friends who over a decade later still had fond memories of spending time in our home.

When Geoff was growing up, our house was the go-to place for the neighborhood kids. Weekday afternoons and Saturday mornings would find them crowded into our family room, playing video and board games and making up their own fun along the way. Laughter and the smell of freshly baked, made-from-scratch chocolate chip cookies filled the air. When Cari baked cookies, word got out quickly, and knocks on the door happened moments apart.

We wanted it that way. It helped us stay close to our kids and their friends, who all went to the schools nearby. We reasoned that the longer we were able to be part of their world and have a positive influence on it, the better.

But distance comes naturally with time. As children mature they seek their independence, and we find ourselves having to let go little by little, no longer able to make their decisions for them. So we guide them as best we can—all the while hoping and praying they will make the right choices.

High school was like that. When Geoff started, he showed signs of progress. It looked like he had learned from his mistakes in middle school and was heading into a new place and a new year with added enthusiasm. Each new school year always seemed to start with hope.

That hope died before the semester ended. Telltale signs that something was wrong slowly made their way to the surface out of the troubled depths:

"Are you going out for lacrosse this year, Geoff? Riverside has such a good team."

"Nah, Dad. The other kids are better, and I wouldn't get a chance to play."

"But aren't you going to at least try?"

"I don't think so. I'm just not as interested in it as I used to be."

It was an honest answer. Geoff was a freshman, and competition for the team was intense. And I knew that if I pushed him too hard, my efforts would be rebuffed and any chance of his trying out for the team would be lost.

What I didn't know was that his love for lacrosse was waning as his interest in drugs was increasing. We didn't know this because he hid it well. But an unsettling sense that something was wrong began to grow in us. Geoff spent less time with kids from the neighborhood—kids he had been close to since elementary school. Plus, he was reluctant to introduce us to his new friends. At first, we thought that was just a normal transition into high school.

We soon learned otherwise.

One day we received a call from the main office at school telling us that Geoff was sick. He had passed out that afternoon in class. Drugs were suspected but couldn't be proven (we later learned Geoff had taken pills—synthetic opiates—he had been given by a friend, and his problem was worse than this incident indicated). We had thought that his attending one of the better public schools would encourage him to make healthier choices. Yet it wasn't just that his troubles followed him—he intentionally sought them out.

Not long afterward we found ourselves sitting with a group of parents and children at an intensive outpatient rehab program at Duke University, where Cari worked. It would be the first of many efforts at rehab, and one of the first things we learned was that opioid abuse was occurring at every high school in our community—public and private. In fact, some of the better schools actually had greater difficulty with it (even though it tended to be swept under the rug). Greater affluence sometimes translated into busier and less attentive parents, more idle time, and more money in kids' pockets. Nowhere was safe.

Even though the drug problem was rampant in Durham, the hard fact was that Geoff chose to be a part of it. And the more he pursued it, the deeper his addiction went. It was a vicious cycle that continued to spiral downward.

Geoff seemed to have a predilection toward addiction. There were people who had struggled with alcohol abuse in the past on both sides of our family. Cari's father wrestled with it, as did one of my uncles who died young, plus a great-grandfather. Like Geoff, they made the decision to indulge. But once that choice was set, they lacked an inner "switch" to stop—they simply liked it too much.

I was wired differently and had difficulty understanding Geoff's tendencies. When I was in high school in the seventies in California, I had "friends" who tried to get me to drink at parties or smoke weed—and I later learned that sometimes they took bets that they could. I never gave in—even though it cost me in popularity. Still, I was voted "most likely to succeed" by my senior class, and I became the state champion in informative speaking that same year.

I expected Geoff to be the same way—driven to succeed and able to just say "no." I naively took for granted that he would make the same choices I had—he was, after all, my son. But when he didn't, I churned inside.

The questions kept coming. Why couldn't Geoff just stop the nonsense and apply himself? Didn't his future matter to him? And why was God allowing this to happen?

After I had tried so hard to do the right thing at his age, it just didn't seem fair. Was God allowing this to teach me to have more patience and compassion? I had to admit I had been overly judgmental at times. Or was I seeing things all wrong? Did my son just need more discipline—the proverbial kick in the pants?

Like so many parents of prodigals, we found ourselves hurled by our new circumstances into emotional extremes. One day would be up, and the next day would be abysmal. I loved my son and wanted to help him. But just when it seemed as if he was making progress, he would fall back again.

Still, there were good days, days that helped us keep our sanity and hold on to hope. There were seasons when Geoff seemed to get a handle on his problem, and his stellar gifts and abilities would shine. We'd see "him" again—not the hard-edged, gangster wannabe version that drug abuse had twisted him into. There was even a period when Geoff's childhood faith began to emerge again, and he was making progress in it. He professed faith in Christ and was baptized.

But eventually the storms would appear on the horizon again.

As a pastor, I took seriously my responsibility to shepherd my family in their faith, and I did my best to stay consistent between home and church. I didn't want my children to see a father who was one thing on Sunday morning and something different behind closed doors during the week.

We were fortunate to have an understanding board of elders who loved our family and walked closely with us. As I opened up about what we were going through, they listened with compassion and concern. When I pondered resigning because of our circumstances, they walked with us through the painful seasons. Some had personal experience with substance abuse in their immediate or extended families in past years. They prayed with us and for us, and they held me accountable to do my best to love and discipline Geoff and point him to God. They also recognized the spiritual implications of the battle we were in and the ways our adversary was using this to undermine our work together in planting a church.

Once or twice there was a church member who wasn't aware of these efforts and would judge from a distance with a critical spirit, but overall there was genuine understanding that we were trying to walk faithfully through difficult circumstances.

One day after a family meeting in rehab, one of the counselors pulled me aside. "When you're the parent of an addict," she said, "it's hard for others to understand. If your child were sick or had another problem, people would bring meals to your door and listen sympathetically. But when your child is an addict, you don't get a casserole."

The struggle with addiction is often long and drawn out—for addicts and for those who love them. But it is love that is needed most of all. Cari understood this better than I, and it seemed to come naturally to her. Years of praying for an alcoholic father and loving him in spite of his poor choices had taken the edge off her attitude and words, and they taught her a patience I had yet to learn. She was able to celebrate even the smallest victory and to be encouraging when she saw even a slight step in the right direction. She was also slower "to anger" (James 1:19 ESV) than I was. But that sometimes made for tension between us—times when she felt I was too harsh, and I didn't feel she was being hard enough. Tension between parents can be frequent when your child takes a prodigal path. It's easy to differ on how to respond to difficulties, and to make matters worse, sometimes a prodigal will use those differences for personal advantage.

I was also wrestling with legalism. I knew that Jesus had every solution Geoff needed, but I was so bothered by the choices my son was making that I had trouble getting beyond them so I could point him to Jesus in love. Time and again when I tried to talk about faith, I found myself tripping over dos and don'ts. I wanted to see the fruit of faith in Geoff's heart, but the tree hadn't been planted.

It was love that Geoff responded to best of all. If he sensed that our motives were loving, we could still reason with him. He knew we had a zero-tolerance policy for substance abuse and that he would be spontaneously drug-tested (with consequences) at home and in rehab. He also knew and accepted that we would monitor his cell phone and his computer. But as time went on, he would find ways around it. One day Cari was looking out the kitchen window when she saw one of the neighborhood kids hide something at the end of our driveway. She went out to investigate, and she found a freshly filled urinalysis drug test vial. Geoff had given him the vial, and he had filled it to help him avoid being caught. We intercepted it moments before Geoff did.

Problems continued at school and at home, and as winsome as Geoff was, he couldn't always charm his way out of them. He left one high school after a year and went to another, hoping to make a new beginning yet again. But one day during his junior year he was caught smoking weed with friends behind the church across the street from the school. After other offenses, he found himself at the continuation (sometimes called alternative) school. And in spite of increased surveillance, personal searches, and other preventive measures there, he still pushed the limits. One day he was caught with a bag of fifteen Xanax and was charged with trying to sell them.

He went directly to jail and we let him stay there, hoping that would bring him "to his senses" (Luke 15:17). Later, the principal at his second high school opted to give Geoff another chance. But when he was caught with several Ecstasy pills some months later, he was expelled again. There would be more time in rehab, an expensive date in court where he narrowly avoided a felony drug charge, and a continued financial burden on the family. He had now burned his bridges with the local schools, so I homeschooled Geoff to help him complete high school.

Again and again, we found ourselves pushed to the end of our strength. And as that brought us to our knees, in time we would discover it was the best place for us to be.

GEOFF

Don't preach the gospel to someone with slit wrists.
DERMOT GIBNEY

I leaned back and pressed on my eyes until I saw colors. They were sore from the blue light radiating from the computer screen. I wasn't sure what time it was, but I could hear birds chirping outside my bedroom window.

Nights like these were frequent. I would get lost in a world of information, and I couldn't turn my brain off after being fascinated by story after story. I had peers who experienced something similar when it came to certain subjects they loved or maybe even Scripture they couldn't put down, but for me it wasn't anything academic or spiritual.

I had developed an unquenchable fascination with drugs. I loved them. Not just how they made me feel but the seemingly endless possibilities of what could be and where my brain could go. I would stay up all night searching forums and websites—reading about how various substances made people feel and wanting to experience it myself.

Over time, I saturated myself in stories of people experimenting with different combinations of drugs. Pharmaceuticals, psychedelics, stimulants, benzos—I read about them all. As I absorbed more experiences, I became desensitized to what they were describing. I no longer had the least fear of trying any drug or any method of doing drugs; after all, my "friends" on the internet had survived. I could too. Not only did I lack a fear of drugs but I also longed for access to more of them.

It is ironic how the community around me and the stories I read brought me into a lifestyle. I knew the church community, so this was just a replacement for that. The community of addicts I was a part of online was like my church, their stories were my Bible, and the drugs were my god. I had the zeal of a new believer, and there was nothing I wouldn't do.

The only thing that interrupted my study of drugs was getting ready to head to school in the morning. I didn't mind school; I actually loved it. I saw it as an opportunity to find what I was looking for—but I would rarely go to class. I spent my time net-working, meeting people, and asking around where I could find various substances. The high school I was attending had a repu-tation for housing all sorts of drugs. You just had to find them, and it didn't take me very long to do that.

"What's good? You know where I can get something?" I whispered across the aisle to a seedy-looking kid who was half asleep in the back row of my US History class. "What kind of something?" he hissed back at me. "I don't care, whatever you got," I said. I figured if anyone was going to have drugs on them at school, it was definitely this kid. He had shaggy brown hair and a Rasta-colored hoodie that most kids affectionately referred to as a drug rug. "Dude, I don't even know you. You can't just go around asking stuff like that," he warned me.

There was truth to what he said. I knew a few people at school, but none of them were the type of people I wanted to know. There was a subculture to be found, but it turns out the way to find it wasn't asking for a pill the way you would ask about Girl Scout cookies. Nevertheless, I persisted in my search and slowly broke my way in. I knew the dialect, dressed the part, and had no social anxiety when it came to asking around.

Not everyone I met tried to find drugs with the same intentionality I did. For the average kid it was an opportunistic thing: wrong place, wrong people, wrong time. It seems as though that was the majority of people I used with, and something about my desperate search scared people. Slowly, the few positive influences I had in my life began to fade away—replaced with new friends.

This new cohort of mine spent their time in the woods behind our school. There was a trail that went down to a local river, and this made it easy to skip class. So it came to be that I would rarely set foot in the school building. Instead, I would automatically head down to the river with my friends. That was a daily ritual for us, but one day the school's resource officer caught wind of it. He came down and dragged us all into the principal's office. It was a quick chastisement and less trouble than I had been in before. When I was given a few days of in-school suspension (ISS), it hardly affected me.

When the next day came, I wandered into the ISS room and plopped down at a desk. The school was adding new space, so for the time being ISS took place in a trailer behind the school. It was freezing cold in there, and you would spend the day watching time drip off the clock like sap out of a tree. Nothing moved slower than that clock.

"Psst, hey dude, remember me?" I heard someone say under his breath. I turned around and saw my acquaintance from earlier that week in US History. "Yeah, I remember you. What are you doing in here?" I inquired while admiring the stench of burnt weed that wafted off his hoodie. Little to my surprise, he too had gotten caught skipping class in the woods. "Well, at least now I know you're cool. You wanna take something that'll make you feel all weird?" he asked as he motioned up and down with his hands attempting to show me what weird felt like.

He discreetly slid a pill toward me when no one was looking. I scooped it up and popped it in my mouth. I didn't need to waste time asking what it was or where he got it. I knew I would take it no matter what. There was nothing better to do anyway. We were supposed to sit there and stare at the wall all day, so I figured the pill would make the time pass a bit easier.

"Everybody up!" I heard from the front of the classroom. "It's time to go to lunch!" We got up, sauntered into line, and then marched to the cafeteria like a chain gang heading out to work. If you were in ISS, you got lunch last. We had to wait till the last kid got his tray of square pizza and soupy collard greens before we could step up and receive ours. It was supposed to be some sort of punishment—as if they wanted kids to point their fingers and shout, "Shame on you!" as we waited for our lunch.

To me it was a badge of honor.

I sat and choked my lunch down while I remarked to my new friend, "Dude, I really don't feel anything." At the time it was true. I was expecting more from the little pill he had slipped to me. Then slowly but surely it began to take hold. My head got light, I couldn't talk normally, and before I knew it, I hit the ground.

I don't remember much from that day, but I will never forget the week that followed. After being brought home by my parents that day, I was in a strange state of mind. All I wanted to do was be alone, so I begged and begged to leave the house. My parents wouldn't let me go. I got so frustrated and caught up in what I wanted to do that I threatened them in an attempt to get out.

I was finally able to leave the house, but it wasn't in the way I wanted. Instead, I was put in the local psych ward for a week. I didn't know it then, but this would be the beginning of many times when I would be confined against my will.

The psych ward was a difficult place for me to be. I couldn't smoke cigarettes, didn't have access to my drugs, and lived on someone else's schedule. It was there that I remember realizing just how far my obsession with drugs had gone. I could not live sober. I hated being in my mind, hated not feeling some altered state of consciousness, so I did what I could to fool myself into being intoxicated.

There were other drug obsessed kids with me at the psych ward, and we would spend most of our time recounting drug stories and trying to find ways to get high. We were told that LSD was stored in your spine and if you cracked your back, it may trigger a hallucination flashback. We tried that. We also heard that you could grow a mold on fruit peels covered in toothpaste that had psychoactive properties. We tried that as well. Our insanity knew no bounds.

After a week passed, I finally got out, and I was taken to see a substance abuse counselor. His name was Gary, and I grew to enjoy visiting him. He was honest with me, and he had been where I was himself. He never condemned me but always gave it to me straight. Gary became a big part of my family's life over time. He often served as a mediator between my parents and me. I also began to attend his Intensive Outpatient Program, which served to keep me sober in short bursts of time.

Gary tried to play a role in reconciling my parents and me. It was no easy task, as the distance between my parents and me had grown deep. Our relationship had begun to fall apart, and my father had tried all sorts of ways to mend it.

He would sit me down and try to look me in the eyes as I did my best to cast my gaze elsewhere. With all the sincerity in the world he would ask me to consider my choices and what I was doing. He tried all sorts of different tactics to get me to stop:

"Do you know you can kill yourself?"

"Do you know how this looks, and how it reflects on our family?"

"You won't do anything with your life if you continue down this path."

"We raised you better than this."

"I love you. Please don't do this."

"Those kids aren't your real friends."

He made so many appeals, but the one he used most was his faith. He would beg me to consider God's opinion, ask me to pray or read my Bible, or he would quote verses to me that he had read that day. He bought me books, CDs—pretty much any Christian propaganda (as I saw it then) in the hope that it would help me see the truth. Very little made a difference.

The strange thing about that time is that I believed in God, and I agreed with the Scripture that was put before me. I had confessed my faith and had been baptized by my father in the local river after a church service scant years before.

But I didn't make a connection between my faith and my lifestyle.

No one could convince me there was anything wrong with doing drugs. I went to church, I knew the Bible, and then after Sunday I would go get high. I just enjoyed it.

The relationship between my father and me had been crushed—crushed under the weight of my lifestyle, his formidable faith, and both of our expectations. Every moment we were together turned into an appeal one way or the other. The time we used to spend simply being together—playing video games, walking in the woods, playing paintball—had been replaced by arguing, pleading, and storming off.

My father was so concerned with getting me to God that he forgot to maintain our relationship, and I was so concerned with hiding my actions that I refused to let him in. It was a cycle that went back and forth, lumping blame on both sides—and eventually we just gave up. We gave up on having a relationship, and we gave up on spending time together. It was too difficult to constantly battle with each other.

I remember feeling like I had to check out every time my father came to talk to me. I knew that he was just going to hurl another verse at me or try to pray for me. I rarely would even listen to the words he said because I thought it was so predictable.

What really would have surprised me was if my parents would have just stopped with the evangelizing and simply spent time with me. Put aside quoting Bible verses and play some video games or toss a frisbee around. If they would talk, joke, laugh, or have fun even when it is difficult.

While my parents may have made mistakes in their approach with words, their actions more than redeemed them. No matter how hard I would push them away, they would always be there loving me, supporting me, and pushing me in the right direction. They weren't perfect in any way, but they were present no matter what. Eventually—much later—I would begin to see their love, and they were able to speak truth into my life in a beautiful way until it ultimately landed. And only later would I discover how much prayer played a role in what my parents were trying to do to bring me back.

4

"TODAY WAS A GOOD DAY"

JAMES

*The blessing which costs us the most
prayer will be worth the most.*
CHARLES H. SPURGEON, *SPURGEON'S SERMONS ON PRAYER*

Whenever a day would go without drama, Cari and I found ourselves saying, "Today was a good day." It became a cherished phrase for us, something we'd repeat reassuringly now and then to each other. It was code for "Today was a day with no police cars in the driveway, no arrests, no phone calls, no drugs."

The problem our family was facing with drugs loomed so large it seemed to be everywhere. Temptation was all around Geoff. Even if he changed his school or his friends, it followed wherever he went. And the debate over the legalization of marijuana that was playing out in the popular culture just added fuel to the fire. "God made it," Geoff liked to argue. "Why shouldn't it be okay?" "God also made hemlock," I quipped, darkly. "That doesn't mean you should take it."

Messages in music and the media enforced Geoff's thinking that it was okay for him to use marijuana, and he caricatured anyone who opposed it as uptight and uninformed. Then there were the cool parents who looked the other way with a wink and a nod while their kids and their friends used. Even a recent president of the United States had confessed to smoking weed—he just said that he "didn't inhale"—and the reasoning *du jour* seemed to be, "If you can smoke pot and still grow up to be president, what harm could it cause?"

Still, we knew pot had a destructive effect on our son because we knew him better than anyone else. We had seen it in so many ways—an increasing interest in chasing highs, decreased motivation for school, a lack of interest in his future, and a marked aggression a couple of days later that would cause him to slam his fist into a wall at the slightest period after provocation. (Links between cannabis and aggression, while often overlooked because of the drug's initially calming effects, are becoming increasingly evident. One study of 12,000 American high school students determined that those who smoked pot were more than three times as likely to become violent.)[3]

We had to stay on top of Geoff constantly, continuing with in-home drug tests and enforcing consequences—but it felt as if the world was against us—and if the truth be told, it was. God's words to Cain described Geoff's struggle well: "Sin is crouching at your door; it desires to have you, but you must rule over it" (Genesis 4:7).

These day in, day out challenges with our son increasingly brought us to the point where we understood that we couldn't bring about change in Geoff's life in our own strength, no matter how hard we tried. He had to want that to happen.

One day, Gary, Geoff's counselor in intensive outpatient rehab, gave us this advice: "You can lead a horse to water. You can't make him drink. But you can make him thirsty." By that he meant that we had to continue to hold Geoff accountable and use whatever means we could to encourage him to want to make a change. But Geoff was stubborn by nature, and his ongoing struggle with addiction only exacerbated that trait.

As much as we wanted to, we couldn't change Geoff's heart. But we still had to try. We had to reason with him and do our best to persuade him to want a better life. The heart work that needed to happen could only be worked out between Geoff and God.

One of the upsides of the challenges we were facing with Geoff was that they forced us to try to live increasingly in the moment with God. A quiet desperation drove us to prayer day after day. We held on to the hope that God could change Geoff's will even if he didn't want Him to. God had ways of reaching inside Geoff that we couldn't begin to understand. Where our reasoning failed, God would know the way.

But how do you pray on those days when you're all prayed out—when you've gone over the same things so frequently in your prayers that you've run out of things to say to God? On a bad day, you can wonder if your prayers make any difference at all or if they're even being heard. But the prayer "How long?" occurs again and again in Scripture (Psalms 13, 35, 79, 89; Habakkuk 1; Revelation 6). So we came to understand that God wanted us to also pray our questions and weaknesses—to bring it all to Him. Real prayer isn't about having to get the words right or having your act together so you're somehow "good enough" to approach God. It's about a relationship with Someone who already loves us more than life itself and bends with compassion to meet us in our mess.

We began to discover that the more we prayed, the more the good days somehow seemed more frequent, even if it was only our perspective that changed and little else. We found ourselves more able to cope with the unexpected; God was at work within us in new ways, deeper ways, meeting us in the moment with His peace. It was practical and comforting beyond words.

Hope and trust in God's character and kindness increasingly motivated us to reach for what He alone could do in Geoff. We began to look for promises in God's Word that we could appropriate for our own situation. The nineteenth-century British preacher Charles Spurgeon said, "Nothing so fully fixes the course of action of the Lord our God as His own promise . . . . God has bound Himself to be true to His Word."[4] No matter how badly Geoff (or we) had messed things up, we clung to the truths that God's mercies are still "new every morning" (Lamentations 3:23) and that "no matter how many promises God has made, they are 'Yes' in Christ" (2 Corinthians 1:20).

God's Spirit moves through His Word unlike any other place, and we ran there for comfort and calm—especially on difficult days. We'd go there to be in God's presence and to find fresh mercy for the day (Lamentations 3:22–23). I eventually found myself writing my prayers and intertwining them with promises I found, addressing specific concerns we were facing with Geoff.

Those thoughts were the beginnings of my book *Prayers for Prodigals* (see appendix A). Working on that book became an act of devotion and a vital part of my praying for my children. And the more I would write and pray, the more I felt as if I wasn't really doing the writing. Thoughts and verses sometimes came so easily that it seemed as though God was carrying me, giving my own prayers wings.

One day as I wrote, I had a mental picture of all the attacks the adversary had aimed at our family. Those attacks seemed to be heading in our direction like hundreds of black, flaming arrows out of the sky. I imagined myself reforging those arrows on the anvil of God's Word. Then I saw the sky filled again with these reforged arrows—now gleaming silver, headed back in the opposite direction. There were thousands of them, filling the air.

The thought brought me to tears; it was as if I were seeing the prayers of thousands of believing parents, a battle-hardened army bent on taking back someone precious who had been stolen from them by the devil. We could do nothing in our own strength, but through God, all things are possible (Matthew 19:26). One of the prayers that expressed this increasing dependence is found in Day 10 of *Prayers for Prodigals*[5] (which uses the 1984 NIV):

BRING THE BOY TO ME

"O unbelieving generation," Jesus replied, "how
long shall I stay with you? How long shall I
put up with you? Bring the boy to me."
MARK 9:19

Here he is, Lord.
This is my son, and he needs you desperately.
I bring him to you, all that he is and all that is going on
    in his life.
His life is beyond my power to repair or set right.
I ask you to touch him and help him, Lord!
Years ago when you told the disciples, "Bring the boy to
    me," you began the greatest blessing of the child's life.
Darkness had to flee. It could not stand in your presence.
So I bring my son into "the light of your presence" again
    today (Psalm 89:15).
I'm reminded of what you told your disciples.
The child could be set free "only by prayer" (Mark 9:29).
The disciples had tried everything they could think of, but
    no matter how hard they tried in their own strength,
    "they could not" make any difference (Mark 9:18).

You rebuked them for their lack of faith. Then you
said, "Everything is possible for him who believes"
(Mark 9:23).

I'm beginning to understand how much I need to bring
my son to you in faithful, believing prayer.

He needs the difference only you can make for him.

How wonderful that father must have felt when he
walked away with his son, happy and healthy and
standing strong.

He had brought his son to you, and you freed the boy!

Lord Jesus, I look forward to that day in my son's life
as well, the day he meets you and is transformed
by your love, rescued "from the dominion of darkness," and brought "into the kingdom of the Son"
(Colossians 1:13).

What a day that will be!

There will be "rejoicing in heaven" (Luke 15:7) and if
I'm still here, on earth as well!

By faith I see it coming, and I pray that day will come
soon.

I believe you will save my son, and that nothing will
stand in your way!

I look forward to that moment when "the day dawns and
the morning star rises" in his heart (2 Peter 1:19).

Please, Lord, could that day be today?

It is sometimes said that "You're only as happy as your saddest
child." But through prayer, we began to discover a new and quiet
strength and contentment in God that was greater than our circumstances. Cari and I also began to fast together as we prayed
for our family. It would usually be on a Thursday when both of
us were at work. We would skip lunch and take the extra time we
would've spent eating to bring our needs before God.

Sometimes those days praying would bring lasting progress. Other times it seemed like nothing would happen at all. But that caused us to wonder what would have happened if we hadn't prayed. In spite of his struggles, Geoff was able to stay the course with homeschooling and increasingly began to have clean drug screens. He finished high school at home and began to take courses at a local community college. He was beginning to seem more like himself again.

Still, challenges continued. Geoff would advance and then slip up again. Sometimes we'd find him selling things to friends—like video games he had recently purchased, and we knew he still wanted drugs. Sometimes cash disappeared from his sister's room. I found myself buying a safe to keep valuable items out of sight and out of reach. Hard conversations followed each incident: "Don't you believe me, Dad?" But all I could muster in response was: "I want to believe you." That was difficult for Geoff to hear.

In spite of the tension and missteps, Geoff was still moving forward step-by-step. With high school and some community college courses behind him, he began to consider options for his future, and we tried to encourage him wherever we could.

One of the questions that loomed large was, "What kind of school would accept him with his record?" Geoff was really bright and tested well, but two different high schools in the same city and continuation school followed by homeschooling told a story that didn't exactly look good on his academic record. This was hard, because Geoff was so capable. It wasn't just a strong will—it was often his intelligence that caused him to question authority and push the limits.

Cari and I had dreams of being at a very different place at this point in our son's life, and that was difficult. We hurt for our son and how his actions would affect his future. There was also probably more self-sympathy in our thinking than we might have cared to admit. We had played by the rules all of our lives, and we felt like we didn't deserve this. We also wrestled with how

God could allow it, because we had tried so hard to be faithful and conscientious parents. This took time to resolve, but because the battle had been so hard-fought we found that God eventually took us to the place where we could celebrate even the smallest victories.

We were simply grateful Geoff was alive and wanting to do better. It wasn't that our expectations were lowered—but they had changed and adapted to the new reality. Questions like, "What career can he pursue?" began to take a back seat to more important things, like "Will he be able to get a handle on this and live a normal life?" Jesus's words defined the moment: "Do not worry about tomorrow, for tomorrow will worry about itself. Each day has enough trouble of its own" (Matthew 6:34).

We were in a struggle for our son's soul. After all, "What good is it for someone to gain the whole world, yet forfeit their soul?" (Mark 8:36) We knew that we loved Geoff deeply—regardless of choices he had made. Even though we were disappointed when our plans for his life didn't work out, we did our best to hold on to the hope that God had a beautiful future for him. And only God could lead us there, day-by-day and step-by-step.

One of the beautiful things God did in that season was to give us deeper encouragement when we prayed with friends. Parents of prodigals desperately need friends who will love them and their child unconditionally and be there for them. Cari and I chose to open up to others, especially other pastors and their wives who had been down a similar path.

Pastor Don was a dear friend. He served a large church in our area and headed a multi-church prayer effort in our city. When I told him what we were going through with Geoff, he gave me a knowing glance. "I've been there," he said thoughtfully. "When my children were little I had a radio show locally. And one day I said that if people simply raised their children according to the Bible, they wouldn't have prodigals. After the show a listener called. She told me about her prodigal, and how she had done her best to honor God in her home and raise her son to believe in Him. But he still rebelled."

Don's voice dropped, and he fought back a tear as he said to me, "I told her, 'Ma'am, I just believe the Word of God.' But years later, I would have a prodigal of my own. Oh, how I wished I could have called her back! But I never got her number. If I had it all to do over again, I would tell her I'm sorry, and I would be careful to judge less and just listen." Don did listen to me that day, and he wept with me as we prayed for our children together.

Cari and I soon would discover that God had many faithful people who had walked this long road and suffered in silence, looking longingly down their children's prodigal paths, waiting for them to return.

Another moment (with another pastor and parent of a prodigal) gave us still more hope. One day, at the close of an evening worship service with leadership from several churches gathered together, a moment of prayer was offered in the front of the sanctuary. Cari and I went forward to pray with another pastor and his wife. We shared the struggles we were going through at home briefly and bowed our heads. After we finished, Keith (the pastor we were praying with) paused and said: "That's interesting. I'm not sure how to put this, but I saw something while we prayed. I saw two arrows flying. And they both turned, and came back. And one came back sooner than the other. I believe that means both children you are praying for will return to God."

Keith didn't know about my thing with arrows. I hadn't mentioned it to him, and it seemed to me to be more than a coincidence. I took the words to heart and thought about them often. They offered the kind of encouragement Cari and I would desperately need in the days ahead.

GEOFF

*The greatness of a community is most accurately measured
by the compassionate actions of its members.*
CORETTA SCOTT KING, JANUARY 2000, ATLANTA, GEORGIA

"Dude, ECU is awesome! You have to come check it out," Matt
told me as we were eating lunch one day. He was a new friend,
but we were like brothers from the start. Matt was one of those
effortlessly cool people who didn't have to try very hard—cool
without even realizing it. A lot of people wanted to be around
him, and so did I.

He had recently left town to attend East Carolina University in
Greenville, just a few hours from Durham. I desperately wanted to
check it out, partly because I thought it would be a good college.
Close enough that I could see my parents but far enough away
that they couldn't just show up. The other part of that desire was
because it had a reputation for being a party school. I thought it
was the perfect place for me.

After I pitched the idea of spending the weekend there like
only the best salesman could, my parents gave in. I had been in a
better spot lately, and they seemed to like Matt. So they sent me
off with all the optimism they could muster. I was excited about
the prospect of going to college, and my parents were as well. I
thought I had finally grown out of heavy drug use and would be
able to control the habits that had landed me in jail time and time
again. We all agreed that a fresh start was something I desperately
needed. This was my chance to be whoever I wanted to be and to
work toward a career of my choosing.

Matt had a large group of friends at ECU, and I fell into the rhythm pretty quickly on my visit there. We spent the weekend together hanging out, and I got a glimpse of what it would be like to attend school there. "I Love College" by Asher Roth was the theme song, and the lifestyle lived up to any university movie fantasy. We didn't do anything completely out of hand, but we went to some parties and spent our time drinking and doing drugs. It was different, I thought, because it wasn't hard drugs. It was the fun stuff that everyone did (or so I thought).

I applied to school there immediately after returning home. I wasn't sure that I would get in, not because of my grades but because of my criminal record. A person with multiple arrests and expulsions wasn't exactly who every college was longing to bring on campus. I waited anxiously to hear back, not sure what to expect. All I knew was that this was my ticket out. It was exactly where I wanted to be. After a long and nervous month, I was pleasantly surprised to receive a packet in the mail. I was accepted!

A few months later my parents dropped me off at my dorm room and bid their goodbyes. I remember it like it was yesterday: Mom crying and hugging me while Dad helped me unpack and gave me final words of wisdom. I rushed them out of the door because I still hadn't gotten over the whole "I don't want people to know my parents exist" thing that high schoolers go through. I hugged them, said a tearful goodbye, and then stood there in my dorm.

A flood of realization swept in: I was totally on my own. I could do whatever I wanted!

Feelings of excitement and nervousness overwhelmed me. I grabbed my skateboard and headed out the door. My dorm was on top of a section of campus called College Hill. I could fly down the road on my skateboard and get almost anywhere on campus in ten minutes. As soon as I could, I headed for Matt's apartment.

"Let's go do something fun," he said when I walked in the door. He clearly had something specific in mind. "I'm down, but I don't have any money," I answered back.

I wasn't accustomed to being able to have fun without paying for something. He assured me that it didn't matter, and we headed off toward campus. I didn't comprehend that he meant there were plenty of ways to make money and lots of drugs and alcohol to be had for free. But we headed off to do exactly that. As I was introduced to this new lifestyle, I was told one phrase over and over: "That's just how it is here."

Free drugs? That's just how it is.

Steal from people? That's just how it is.

Skip class? That's just how it is.

It didn't really matter what we did, I was told that's just how people do things in college. Over time, I needed that reassurance less and less. I adapted well to manipulating people for what I wanted, and I was convinced that the way I was living was the way everyone lived in college.

Of course, this was never true. I had again repeated my mistake of surrounding myself with people who were like me. I sought out people who were interested in using drugs, and they became my only friends. The more I surrounded myself with similar people, the more I was convinced that everyone used drugs in one way or another.

This community would define my time in college. I followed the crowd mindlessly, and I always seemed to choose the wrong crowd. As much as I spent my time taking advantage of the people around me, I also fell victim to many people taking advantage of me. We would steal from each other, sell each other fake drugs, and then make up the next day to do it all over again. The majority of my relationships were parasitic. The only reason I would spend time around someone was if I could gain something from him or her and that sentiment was mutual.

As the months went on, my fresh start began to grow stale. I had come to know a lot of people, and before I knew it I was back to my old habits. Ask around, find whatever drugs I wanted, sell some of them, and use the rest. However, this time it was much easier than it was back in high school. In college, drugs were socially acceptable—almost expected. As time went on, I tried to hold true to my expectation that my opiate habit was gone, but eventually it came creeping back in.

It started small, with a pill here and a pill there. I would take them only if they were available, but I wouldn't seek them out. Then I became accustomed to the feeling again and found myself craving opiates on a regular basis. As I began to use more frequently, I learned how to gain access to large quantities of OxyContin. Previously, I could only find it when someone had a family member who was willing to sell it or had some left over from surgery.

I met a group of people who made trips to Florida to visit the pain clinics that were there. These were also known as "pill mills." My friends would fly or drive down for one day, get an MRI, take it to the clinic, and leave with hundreds, sometimes thousands, of legal, doctor-prescribed pills. The only problem was that they needed the funds for travel. So some friends and I would pool our money, send someone down, and a few days later have all the pills we could ever want. It didn't take long for it to become an everyday habit all over again.

The fresh start, the hopefulness, the excitement, the promises of a future were all important to me, but they were being slowly choked out by my habit. Still, I trusted that this was the beginning of my new life—even as those prospects began to fade. It was always my vision that one day I would grow out of this lifestyle, get a good job, and start a family. That was what continued to propel me forward.

It was like I was wandering through a desert, reaching for some sort of mirage—and every day it was just out of reach. I would make promises to myself and my family about the change that was coming. I thought they didn't understand me or trust that I would be okay one day. They didn't see what I saw. They didn't have the vision that I had. Moreover, they didn't see all the people around me who had similar habits and were still successful students. I would walk the halls and even the grocery stores, telling myself that everyone I saw did drugs in one way or another. How could they not?

While I was at college and being drawn toward a negative community, my parents were experiencing the opposite. As they stressed and lamented about what was happening with their son, people around them loved them and prayed for them. They didn't try to convince them that "that's just who your son is." They believed with them that I would recover, prayed with them that I would be set free. When things seemed hopeless, they wept with them and encouraged them.

5

A FAR COUNTRY

JAMES

*Their joy is all sadness, their mirth is all vain, their
laughter is madness, their pleasure is pain.*
CHARLES WESLEY, "REJOICE EVERMORE WITH ANGELS ABOVE"

When God's love shines in a heart, it shows up on a face. The joy
is perceptible to those who know it—a light behind the eyes that
reveals the life and hope that are ready to spring forth. Once you
see it, you never forget it.

Believing moms and dads look longingly for that light in the
faces of their children. They rely on the light of Christ personally
to get through the day, and they pray for it in the hearts of those
they love. They understand it to be their children's greatest need

in life—the one gift they would give them if only they could. They know that "the light shines in the darkness," and the darkness will never "overcome it" (John 1:5). Life can be hard, but it's so much harder without God and His light.

Looking back on pictures of Geoff from the time of his deepening addiction, I see the absence of light. That too is perceivable. There was an emptiness behind his eyes that betrayed the sadness within. And the irony was that it was the pursuit of happiness and pleasure that landed him there in that empty, lonely place—a place far from God, where darkness stretched its decaying hand deeper within until little more could be seen. As I reflect on Geoff's face in those pictures, T. S. Eliot's famous words come to mind: "We are the hollow men . . . The eyes are not here / There are no eyes here."[6] Substance abuse would encroach on so many good things in his life like a black hole; he was becoming hollow, and he didn't even know it.

The deepest descent began after Geoff left home and went to college, but it didn't happen all at once. We had thought the worst days were behind us. Geoff had made genuine progress in stepping away from substances. The summer before he left was upbeat and positive—at last he was moving on with his life! Mistakes made in high school hadn't kept him out of college, and best of all, he wanted to go. He was interested in bettering his life and making choices that would benefit his future. What parent wouldn't love that?

We spent the summer getting him ready, making sure he had everything he needed for a good beginning: laptop, notebooks, clothes. We visited the college together and came away hopeful. Geoff enrolled online early and found several classes he liked.

Before he left for college, we talked about the new chapter he was starting in his life and the temptations he would face. Geoff was confident, but he was also young—younger than most he would be sharing classes with. Yet Cari and I were assured he was sincere in his assertion that he had no desire to get messed up with drugs again. Even though ECU had a reputation for being a party school, we knew Geoff would encounter that almost anywhere in college, and we thought his past experiences were helping him grow beyond that. Perhaps our wanting this to be true made us less circumspect than we should have been. Geoff was taking on new responsibilities and was shouldering them well, and we were glad to see it. We would miss him, but we were grateful that he was leaving Durham and many of its negative influences behind. It looked like he was growing up.

Geoff had always been gifted socially; he meshed well with people and made friends quickly. But this was also his Achilles' heel. He was young and impressionable and easily influenced, and relationships with others who struggled in the same ways he did could take him downhill quickly. So we encouraged him to find a church, read his Bible daily, be careful in his friendships, make academics a priority, and call—always call—if he ever found himself in over his head.

The call came sooner than we expected. However, we didn't recognize it as the cry for help that it actually was. There are moments in a parent's life when you look back and wish you had done things very differently. You replay it over in your head, and the same sinking feeling always comes with it: *Why hadn't I seen then what was so obvious now?* Few things hurt worse than knowing you weren't there for your child when he needed you to be.

Geoff called on a weekday evening. He had closed the door to a bathroom in his apartment so his roommates wouldn't hear him, and he was in tears. College wasn't what he expected, and he wanted to come back. Things were more difficult than what he had imagined, and he missed home so much more than he ever thought he would.

We listened. Then we told him he should stay.

To us it sounded like he was just homesick, and because Cari and I had both been through that our first year away at college we thought it was just a transition he was going through. But there were deeper undertones. What we were missing—and what Geoff wasn't telling us—was that he was beginning to struggle with the same temptations he had before. There were too many parties, and because he was already well-liked he was invited to lot of them. He wanted to be accepted by others; as a result, he was beginning to fall back into old ways and make choices he shouldn't have.

But this time it was worse. The college *Animal House* culture seemed to give everything an air of acceptability—drinking too much, casual sex, smoking pot, an occasional pill—"it's just what people do." And Geoff, always the risk-taker, would take it to an extreme.

He lasted a semester. Still, we didn't really grasp what was happening. We wanted to believe that all was well. When he called and told us he could save money by leaving the university and going to the local community college there in Greenville for a few semesters, we didn't hesitate. Geoff, like most addicts, was becoming a master manipulator—and we were clueless.

Within two semesters Geoff's substance abuse would take an even harder turn. To further his habit with pills, he had been selling them on the side. Then he started selling heroin. Due to his old habits and haunts he learned about in Durham, he had no problem going to parts of Greenville that other college students would avoid. The suppliers loved it because he was opening new territory for them. But one day he ran out of money and couldn't find any pills.

He was starting to get sick from withdrawal. At the time, he had a girlfriend who grew up in Baltimore and was no stranger to substance abuse. She had a brother who shot up heroin and suffered consequences for it—and because she did, Geoff told us she was deeply opposed to drugs because she had seen what they can do. It was a lie. While we thought she would be a positive and safe presence in his life, years later Geoff would disclose that she abused opiates herself. When Geoff ran out of pills but had heroin left over to sell, her response was, "Why don't you just try some of this?"

It was all the excuse he needed. The bridge was crossed. Geoff had gone from pot, to pills, to intravenous heroin abuse. Like the prodigal in Luke 15, he had lost his senses and stepped foot in the far country. He never imagined he would take the road so far. And to Cari and me, it was absolutely unthinkable.

But we were about to find out.

GEOFF

He who makes a beast out of himself gets rid of the pain of being a man.
DR. SAMUEL JOHNSON, *ANECDOTES OF THE REVD. PERCEVAL STOCKDALE*

I could barely hold my hands still as I prepared my first shot of the day. They were shaking uncontrollably, and my entire body was covered in sweat. But I was freezing cold. I was on the verge of throwing up, and my heart was pounding inside my chest. This was nothing new.

Every morning was like this. My first coherent thought of the day was always how to make it stop. To feel better, I did the same routine every day: wake up early, grab my phone, and call my dealer.

I had meant to save a little heroin for this morning, but my self-control failed somewhere around 2 a.m., as it always did. Leftover heroin saved for later was an imaginary thing.

I was sitting in a grimy restroom stall inside a gas station. I carefully balanced my kit on top of the toilet: a cap from a bottle of soda, a cotton swab, and a dull syringe that had already been used several times. I dumped the contents of three wax bags into the cap and stuck the syringe into the toilet to get the small amount of water I needed. It was gross, but sanitation was the least of my worries in that moment. It was just like tap water, I told myself. I did my best to hold still, squirted the water into the cap, mixed the solution up with the plunger of my syringe, dropped a piece of the swab in the liquid to use as a filter, and pulled the liquid up into the syringe.

I quickly ripped off my belt, pulled it tight around my arm and began the search for a vein. This part was the worst: Knowing that sweet relief was right around the corner and not being able to find a vein that was still functioning. I jabbed myself repeatedly—causing bruises and making blood drip down my arm. And then I finally saw it. The red mist shot up the needle into the brown solution. I pressed down the plunger and a metallic taste filled my mouth. You could always somehow taste it when it hit your veins.

The feeling came rushing in like a freight train. That was what I needed. Oblivion. Nothingness. A warm blanket pulled over my entire body that subdued all the pain, frustrations, and promises of the day. I let out a breath, and slowly my eyes began to close.

"What the heck, man! You've been in there forever! What are you doing?" the gas station attendant yelled through the door of the bathroom. I was sprawled out on top of the toilet and wasn't exactly sure where I was or how long it had been. I slapped myself awake, gathered my kit, put my belt back on, unlocked the door, and trudged out to the parking lot.

There was a line of people waiting outside the restroom, and they all looked pretty angry. People glared at me, but I was used to it. My unfastened belt, clammy skin, and track marks down my arm confirmed their suspicions. I didn't care, though. I had gotten exactly what I needed. As I fell into the driver's seat of my SUV and started the car up, I realized how high I was. I'm just glad I didn't overdose, I thought to myself. I had hit the perfect line that every junkie searches for—as far into delirium as you could get without dying. I glanced down at my phone and saw several text messages and a lot of missed calls.

"Hey man, where you at?" "Are you good?" "Call me as soon as you get this!" All of the text messages had a similar urgency as people were searching for their next high. The only reason anyone called me anymore was for mephedrone. People were beginning to plan their evenings and wanted to have fun.

A friend of mine had gotten hold of this new drug before anyone else in our city. It was the start of the synthetic analogue craze that swept the nation back around 2010, and we were ahead of the game. Most of these drug analogues were not illegal yet, and some were even sold in stores. The most commonly used one was referred to as "bath salts." We received it in the mail from overseas, loaded it in small capsules for storage, and sold it to anyone who would buy (there was no shortage of customers).

I spent the majority of the day driving around making deliveries and earning money—money that would go toward one thing: heroin. I didn't waste my time or money using any other drugs. My desire to have a variety of psychonautic experiences had given way to an insatiable appetite for IV heroin. I knew what I wanted and pursued it day and night. I officially dropped out of ECU and was attending the local community college, but I rarely went—only when I was high enough to want to go sit in class for an hour. I would dream of having millions of dollars and kilos of heroin. I thought if I could just achieve that, then I would be okay. I couldn't be more wrong. The more money I had, the more dope I did. I was careening toward the grave and leaving a path of destruction in my wake.

In reality, I was barely keeping myself afloat. I had dealers who would front me drugs to sell; I would use most of them and then sell small amounts to barely pay back my balance. I bounced my debt back and forth between dealers like this was an expert Ponzi scheme. I would borrow drugs from one person, consume it all, and then borrow more from another person and sell it to pay back the first. There were many times when I would do the math wrong or use too much and have to figure out how to pay back substantial sums of money to keep myself in good standing. It was a risky, wild practice, and it was my daily life.

This time around, I had done it again—used too much of my stash to pay back a dealer. Now I was scrambling to make it up. I had run the gamut of dealers and no one else would trust me, so it was time to figure something else out. I decided to resort to one of my normal tactics, which ranged from selling fake drugs to robbing people to breaking into houses. I racked my brain thinking through where I could find a considerable sum of money. A couple hundred dollars wasn't going to get me out of it this time.

A good friend of mine had recently moved to Greenville, and I had spent a lot of time with him over the past few weeks. I remembered that he had an affinity for hunting, which goes hand in hand with a collection of expensive weaponry. Guns were constantly in high demand in the circles I ran in, and I knew that I could solve all my problems with one score. My lifestyle had earned me a desperateness that left no one off-limits when it came to theft, not even my best friends or family. As I drove over to his house, I thought about the consequences I could face. I was torn about committing this theft, but at the end of the day, there were no other choices. I told myself I was just going over there to hang out, but in the back of my mind I knew that if he was absent I would leave there with one of his guns.

I knocked on his door and there was no answer. I went to the back and was surprised to find the sliding glass door unlocked (you'll recall that I had done this dance before). I assured myself with some strange sort of comfort that if I was not the one who broke in, eventually someone else would. I padded through the doorway, grabbed his AR-15, rolled it in a blanket, tossed it in the back of my SUV, and tore out of the driveway before anyone could notice.

I quickly called an acquaintance who would be interested in purchasing the gun. Normally, I would take the time to file off the serial numbers so it couldn't be traced, but I was too excited to be cautious. I sold the gun that evening, paid back my dealer, and still had a pretty good chunk of money left over. The rest of the week all blurred together into one long high.

As I squandered what little money was left, I found out that the person I had sold the gun to worked at a legitimate gun store. He had run the serial number and when it came back stolen, he tried to call me and see what was going on. I ignored his calls, figuring he would get over it and move on.

A few days later there was a knock on my door. It was an officer I had come to know very well during my time in Greenville. He worked for the Narcotics Department and had several encounters with me. On one such occasion he had found a small bag of cocaine in my sock. He took me to the police station and told me he would let me off if I would give him information. As usual, I was solely concerned with self-preservation and told him I would turn in every dealer I knew if he would give me some time. However, my lifestyle had engrained a strange sense of honor in me that many addicts tend to have. I would lie, cheat, and steal from anybody, but I would never tell the police a thing.

So for the past few months I had led this officer on a wild goose chase all over Greenville with all sorts of false information that I simply made up every time he called. Needless to say, he wasn't very happy with me, so when he saw my name come across the system on a warrant, he was overjoyed to take me in. He pressed me to see if I knew anything about a stolen gun, and I denied knowing about anything. He stuffed me in the back seat of his car, took me downtown, and locked me in an interrogation room.

We sat in that room and had a battle of wills for hours. I didn't want to admit anything, and he made thinly veiled threats about locking me up and throwing away the key. In my fear, I finally gave in and told him about my theft. I scrawled out a statement, signed it at the bottom, and sealed my fate.

The following week was agonizing. I begged my parents and friends to bail me out but to no avail. The people I thought were my best friends were too busy to care, and my parents were finally seeing through my lies. They were there for me, they talked to me, they told me they loved me; but they would not fall for the same old story again. At the time, I thought it was the end of the world, but in hindsight, I didn't realize how good I had it. My parents had hired a lawyer, and the judge was extremely lenient. I had seen several men with the same charge receive relatively long amounts of time in jail, but I was somehow able to come away with less. The judge gave me time served and ordered me to spend the next thirty days in a rehab facility.

This revelation that I had to spend the next month sober was a relief. I knew I could not last much longer living as I had been, and this was another opportunity to turn my life around. I knew my habit had gotten out of hand, and this would be a great opportunity for change. However, I still couldn't grasp living a life without drugs.

When my time was over, I walked through the metal doors of my pod at Pitt County Jail, and they handed me my belongings: a cell phone, my wallet, and some tattered clothes. I enthusiastically tore off my orange jumpsuit and pulled on my jeans. I walked out of jail that day, and my parents were waiting out front. They had already gone and packed up my things and were ready to take me home for a few days before I went to treatment.

I slid into the back seat of my parents' black sedan, and the leather seat was hot on my skin. My parents greeted me with mixed emotions, unsure of what the future held for me. It was surreal to know I was leaving Greenville behind. I no longer had to maintain the image that I had been putting on for people. But as we pulled out of town that day, I was lulled into another false hope. I thought change was coming. But it was just another dream that I would dash on the rocks of addiction.

6

SQUANDERED NEAR ANGELS

JAMES

But man, proud man, . . . most ignorant of what
he's most assured . . . plays such fantastic tricks
before high heaven as make the angels weep.
WILLIAM SHAKESPEARE, *MEASURE FOR MEASURE*

The facts were staring us in the face—we just didn't want to see them.

Geoff was attending school less, and he had begun to cancel classes he should have passed easily. He didn't sound like himself. Communication with home was increasingly infrequent. Whenever he called he would start with a positive story and turn it into a request for money. His college savings had dwindled unexplainedly, and we felt like we were being played. We wondered if it might be better to have him closer to home.

One day Cari and Geoff's sister made a surprise visit to Greenville, and when they arrived at his apartment in the early afternoon Geoff and his roommates were still sleeping. Remnants from a recent party littered the floor. There were no drugs to be seen, but empty bottles scattered here and there told their tale of the night before. Cari left him with a warning, and she came home deeply discouraged.

One evening just a few days later, Cari and I were sitting in the living room weighing plans to have Geoff come home. The phone rang and a voice we didn't recognize said matter-of-factly, "Will you accept a collect call from Pitt County Jail from a Geoffrey Banks?"

The answer caught in my throat. "What? Um . . . yes."

When the call connected, Geoff's voice was subdued and sad: "Dad . . . Dad. I messed up."

"Oh, Geoff. What did you do?"

"I'm in the county jail here. Can you and Mom come? I'll tell you when you get here."

"All right."

"Dad."

"Yes, son."

"I love you."

"I love you too, son. Goodbye."

One of the constants in our family phone conversations was always to say, "I love you"—no matter how strained our relationships may be. It was one thing Geoffrey had never strayed from—he would always say it and mean it, and it was a helpful reminder in the moment. As soon as I hung up, Cari got online and looked at his charges. They were serious: felony possession and sale of a stolen firearm.

Before we left the next morning, we called an attorney for advice. Then we decided that Geoff would remain in jail until his initial court date. Maybe jail could get through to him in a way we hadn't been able to. We made the trip and waited in line for visiting hours at the jail.

God has a way of putting people in unexpected places when we need them most. After we went through the metal detector into the visitation area, a deputy pulled us aside.

"Mr. and Mrs. Banks? I've been talking with your son. I just wanted to let you know that even though he's here, he's a good kid. He's been having a tough time, but he's been reading a Bible, and some of us are praying for him."

We later found out that a jail chaplain had been having some heart-to-heart conversations with Geoff. Geoff had been having difficulty both physically and emotionally as he was withdrawing from opiates and coming to grips with the potential legal consequences of his actions. For the first time in a long time, he was listening.

It was hard to see him on the other side of the worn and scratched, inch-thick plexiglass. He was wearing an orange jumpsuit, and he looked gaunt and tired. There were dark circles under his eyes, and it was clear he had been crying. Cari and I were having a hard time holding it together ourselves.

In a call before our visit, Cari had already communicated to Geoff that he would be staying there, and to our surprise he didn't argue with us about it. We checked to see if he needed anything and told him we'd put some money on the jail account so he could buy a few things. When our time was up, we told him we loved him and were praying for him, and we left.

Leaving him there was even harder than seeing him at first. Though he was nineteen years old and considered an adult, when your son or daughter is hurting and vulnerable he or she is always your child, no matter what. We wanted to pull him near and comfort him as we had done in years before, but we couldn't touch him. We wanted to speak quietly and reassure him that somehow things would work out. But we didn't have that assurance ourselves in the moment, and we could only shout above the others sitting beside us to be heard through the glass.

Both Cari and I teared up as we walked through the parking lot to the car, and we didn't say much on the long ride home. Still, we were thankful for the encounter with the deputy.

While Geoff was in jail, we had to move him out of the apartment he had shared with friends. He left unexpectedly when he was arrested, and it was in rough shape. Clothes and cans and wrappers were strewn about, the wall had a hole in it, and the door had been broken from someone breaking in. Blacklight and Hendrix posters glared from the wall. As I was cleaning up the bathroom, I discovered a couple of orange colored hypodermic needle casings on the floor. A sinking feeling swept over me; I didn't want to believe they were his.

Before the court date came, we learned that Geoff had gone to a friend's apartment while he was out and had stolen a semi-automatic rifle. He then sold it for cash to further his drug habit. The owner found out about it from a friend, and the weapon was returned. But the county was pressing charges.

Because Geoff had been cooperative in jail and this was his first offense as an adult, the judge was kind to him. If Geoff agreed to extended community service, he would get credit for time served. The charges would be reduced below a felony penalty. We also added another requirement. He had to attend in-patient rehab.

Geoff returned home briefly until a bed was available at a treatment center in Wilmington about three hours away. He was reluctant, but he had no other options.

After a little more than a week at the treatment center, he already wanted out. He began to tell us stories of how others there were breaking the rules and getting away with it. He felt he was being treated unfairly by comparison. Just two weeks later he was out, having tested positive for smoking pot.

We were angry. But his sister, who lived nearby, intervened.

"I know him better than anyone else," she told us. "He can live with me for a while until he gets on his feet. I think I can help him. There's a lot to do in Wilmington besides drugs." We were reluctant to have him return to old ways in Durham, and this was an approach we hadn't considered. We decided to let her try.

He was there for a few months, helping out at a restaurant where his sister worked. Things seemed to be going smoothly at first. Then, after several weeks, some of Geoff's sketchy friends from Durham began to show up wanting to hang out in a city close to the beach. Unbeknownst to her, when Geoff would borrow her car and her debit card under the pretext of filling up the tank, he'd also remove cash from her account and use it to buy heroin. She wasn't watching carefully.

One day she went to withdraw cash from her account, and the card was denied. The balance was zero. Then, when she looked for a roll of cash from tips at work she had hidden at home, it had disappeared. Geoff denied taking it, but everything pointed to him.

His sister was furious and called home immediately: "Dad, Mom, I've kicked Geoffrey out. He can't stay here—not one more night. I found needles in his room. He's an addict, Dad."

The word hit hard. Cari and I were alarmed. "He can't spend the night on the streets down there," Cari said. "Not if his problem is as bad as she says it is. He could get arrested again . . . or worse. I'm going down there to get him today."

I had to stay in Durham and conduct a funeral at the church. Cari made the trip and located Geoff immediately. They packed up what they could and headed home late that evening.

Not many weeks before, Ken, a church elder who was particularly spiritually sensitive and understanding of prodigals, had pulled us aside after the worship service. "I believe we really need to pray for Geoff," he told us. "As I was praying for him this morning God impressed upon me what a spiritual battle this is." Ken was also a chemist and had spent his career investigating illicit substances.

We stepped into the prayer room at the church and bowed our heads. Ken prayed boldly, "Father, please have mercy on

Geoffrey. I ask you to command Satan to leave him alone and to block what he's trying to do in Geoffrey's life. Help him to lose all desire for drugs and bring him back to you, Father. He belongs to you, Father. We look forward to seeing what only you can do, in Jesus's name." Cari and I agreed with him in prayer, touched that he cared so deeply for our son.

Parenting a prodigal in crisis can be like swimming under water. You're constantly under pressure, and you feel like you can only hold out for so long. Communication with God in those moments is difficult and muffled at best. But occasionally, often in the darkest moments, there's a breakthrough. Even though your circumstances don't change, God somehow lifts you above them. Those moments are like oxygen for the soul.

That was what happened the night Cari returned home with Geoff. Geoff had passed out, collapsed like a marionette in the passenger seat beside her. Her heart was aching. How could it come to this? she wondered. How could someone who had so much potential, who had been given so much . . . squander it all, and for what? What would his future be like, where was all of this headed?

The road was empty. Mile rolled on after mile with nothing but the droning hum and click of tires on pavement.

Then she saw them. Four of them, one beside each fender of the car. And suddenly all was silent. The way Cari describes it, she felt as if she was floating, while still being carried along at a constant speed. The car, a heavy older model Mercedes, no longer felt like it was touching the ground.

What she saw were angels. Each looked masculine, but they were all larger than a man, and each one was holding a corner of the car aloft. They flew effortlessly, fast and low, robes aflame with light, faces determined but not threatening—even friendly, somehow. Cari wasn't frightened. She was comforted. They were with her for several miles, from where Highway 147 leaves I-40 until shortly before she exited the freeway five miles from our home.

I know. It could sound . . . made-up. That's what I thought when I first heard it. But you have to understand. Of the two of us, Cari is much more practical. When I have my head in the clouds; she's firmly grounded. My thoughts scatter like confetti in a windstorm; hers are laid out neatly in a row. And in the same clear and cogent way, she insisted that what she saw that night was as real as the ground beneath her feet.

Cari has never seen an angel since, and she had never seen one before that night—which are two of the reasons I believe her. And what she saw that night was enough to bring her through many other nights to come. That night God lifted the veil just long enough for her to see the reality that is around us all the time. "Are not all angels ministering spirits sent to serve those who will inherit salvation?" (Hebrews 1:14).

Geoff may have squandered much, but what happened on that dark highway renewed our hope and gave us the strength and vision to carry on. In spite of all that had happened, God was not far away—"an ever-present help in trouble" (Psalm 46:1). And nothing mattered more than that.

GEOFF

Adolf Hitler is simply the dark side of Mother Teresa.
GREGORY A. BOYD

Nothing seemed real to me until my head hit the pillow that night. Earlier that day my mother had taken me to my first inpatient drug and alcohol rehabilitation center. There was a diverse mix of people here, some as young as eighteen years old and others reaching sixty. I was surprised to learn the myriad of occupations that were represented among my fellow patients. There were police officers, doctors, lawyers, grad students, and soccer moms. There is no specific demographic for addiction. It sinks its hooks into many unsuspecting bystanders who leave the doctor's office with a prescription.

When I checked in that day, I promptly began to socialize and ask people questions. I was genuinely curious if any of the patients here really wanted to change their lives. I had very little context for what residential rehab would be like, and I was unaware that in order to achieve long-term recovery you are urged to quit using all substances. When I heard the counselor mention he had not used any drugs for quite a few years, I scoffed. I did not believe that was attainable, and even if it was, why would you want too? My ideal was to stop being physically dependent on heroin and continue using the drugs I considered less harmful.

After getting checked in, talking to a counselor, having my items searched, and unpacking my things, I was allowed to wander about the campus. I made myself at home, sitting atop a picnic table next to a sand volleyball court that the grass was beginning to take back. I was excited to be in Wilmington. I loved the beach and the idea of living next to it was a comfort amidst so much change.

I lit a cigarette and struck up a conversation with the man seated next to me. He was recently discharged from the US Army and was trying to pull his life back together after an extremely difficult return home. He too had found a paradise in the oblivion that heroin provided. "Are you really trying to stop everything completely?" I asked my new friend. "Yeah, man, I think so. There is so much more to life than living like this," he answered. Somewhere on the inside I knew he was right, but it still did not seem very enticing. A life without drugs and alcohol seemed bland and pointless to me.

When I went to bed that evening, I knew my life was never going to be the same. I was turning into the failure I promised myself and others I would never become. I didn't finish college, I didn't have a good job. I didn't grow out of my addiction or have my own family and a 401k. Instead, I found myself tossing about on a lumpy bed at a treatment center wondering how my life had arrived at where it was.

The next morning we were given time to make phone calls. My parents had provided me with several phone cards so I could make long-distance calls. When they answered the phone, tears began to well up in my eyes. This was the first time I had been sober in years, and the emotions I had caged for so long were beginning to break free. Just hearing their voices made me choke up. I wasn't numbing myself anymore, and I had to face the reality of the things I had done. It was a lot to handle at once, and the dam seemed to break as I continued to speak. After our conversation I told myself I needed a break, so I dialed a friend who lived in Wilmington and convinced him to bring me some relief. Just one small joint—no big deal. I just wanted a one-time relief from the stress and struggle of the day.

It was delayed, but eventually that friend fulfilled his promise. He left a small joint sitting under a rock in the parking lot. So when no one was looking, I skittered out from the side of the treatment center to grab it. We were on a tight schedule at treatment, and I was missing class—but that never mattered to me. I have always struggled with authority, and the biggest consequence I could suffer would be expulsion from a program that I did not want to be a part of.

Everyone was in class at that time except my new ex-military friend and me. When I offered him the prospect of one last smoke, he abandoned his resolve rather quickly. So we crept around the back of the treatment center. We happened upon a small alcove of trees where we thought no one would find us and sparked our small morsel of weed.

About halfway through our session, a counselor who presumably smelled what we were doing came marching down the trail. I blew out the smoke as fast as I could and flicked the joint into the woods. I assured the counselor that it was just a cigarette, but she called my bluff. She angrily took me inside and forced me to take a drug test, which I miraculously passed. Her anger was halted, and I could see that she was questioning her senses.

The next day I could not keep my mouth shut about my small success. I had looked directly in the face of authority and duped them—or so I thought. It was a good feeling to break the rules and get away with it, and it was a tact I would continually pursue. The counselor could not prove anything, and I apparently had gotten away with it—enjoying my high without consequences.

But it turned out that there were some people at the treatment center who were serious about their recovery. They really wanted to progress, so when I bragged about the joint I got away with smoking, they almost immediately told the counselor. Once more I was marched into the bathroom, handed a plastic cup, and required to take a drug test. Now that time had passed, I tested positive for THC (the active chemical in marijuana), and my stay at the treatment center came to an abrupt halt.

The counselors helped me pack my things, and I begged my sister to come pick me up. She graciously agreed to take me into her home in downtown Wilmington, and I was overwhelmed with excitement. I was no longer physically dependent on drugs, and I thought I could just smoke weed and take the occasional pill. I did not know that I would prove myself wrong and go barreling down the well-traveled path back to my addiction.

It didn't take long for me to seek out all the wrong people in downtown Wilmington. I quickly made my way to the sketchiest part of town I could find and boldly asked everyone outside where I could find some "boy" (heroin). After getting robbed twice, I stumbled upon an area that was practically an open-air drug market. In a short time, the drugs had seized control again.

As my habit returned to its previous depths, so did my need for funds. Luckily, my sister was a waitress at the time and kept large amounts of cash from her tips around the house. The temptation proved to be too much for me, and I slowly siphoned off money here and there. As time went on, the amount I had taken surpassed well over a thousand dollars.

I never wanted to hurt her or my family; I never wanted to hurt anyone I stole from. I was just too weak, I thought—too weak to ignore the temptation that always seemed to come my way. I was unaware that over time, my brain chemistry had changed and was telling my body that I needed heroin to survive. Before my need for food, safety, water—the most basic of human needs—I felt like I needed heroin. The mental battle seemed impossible to win.

Once my sister found out about my theft, the doors to her home slammed shut. My parents tried to have me committed to the hospital, calling the police and saying I was a danger to myself and others. But it didn't work. I smooth-talked my way out of it just as I always did and headed back to Durham the same day.

As soon as I arrived back home, I contacted some old friends and got back to business. Even though my parents were watching, I was becoming more skillful at hiding my habit. It seemed that once I had left Durham, heroin became incredibly popular there and most of my friends used it. It was easy to find, and the use became a daily routine once again.

Understanding what I was processing in my brain at that time has proven to be difficult. There is much I do not remember and a lot that I don't understand. The only positive thing that happened is that I stopped feeding myself the lie that I would grow out of my addiction. I knew I wanted to stop, but at the same time I really didn't. I had not had enough consequences yet, and I pressed down the same old path, hoping this time I would find something different. There was a part of me that was open to change, to God, and to something new—but it was as if I had an alter ego that would take over when things became too difficult. This person didn't care about anyone. He had no desire for success or happiness, and the end goal was a drug-fueled rampage toward the grave.

Gary, my old substance abuse counselor, must have caught me on a good day. I had not seen him in years, and I was enlivened at the prospect of catching up. I had a deep respect for Gary, and I knew he understood where I was coming from. He hit me with the same two lines he always did: "Are you just gonna be a junkie for the rest of your life, dude?" and "You're gonna die if you don't stop." He never pulled punches but was incredibly loving and caring at the same time. I appreciated that, so when he told me about a treatment opportunity in Nashville, I listened.

"It is the nicest place ever. I would be willing to spend thirty days there!" he exclaimed. We scrolled through pictures of beautiful, rolling green hills and descriptions of equine therapy and memory foam mattresses. He wasn't lying—the place looked awesome. "It's like summer camp for junkies," he quipped with a big grin on his face. That even made me chuckle. "Not everyone has an opportunity like this. You are really lucky," he told me. At the time I didn't realize how right he was.

I was incredibly fortunate to have the opportunities that I had because of my parents' hard work and insurance. So many people don't have the option to check into detox or treatment centers—they lack money, insurance, or people in their lives who care enough to get them there. I had access to excellent treatment and parents who were willing and able to support me while I was there—yet others die every day because they lack access to resources I took for granted.

That day, after a bit of debate and a lot of questions, I agreed to go to junkie summer camp. Somehow the side of me that wanted to get better seemed to be more in control during those days. I finally accepted that I would have to aim for full sobriety and that I could not continue using what drugs I deemed as okay. With a returned sense of optimism, my parents bid me farewell and prayed desperately for what would come next. God was slowly piecing together His mosaic.

7

A Tougher Love

James

How well I have learned that there is no fence to sit on
between heaven and hell. There is a deep, wide gulf, a
chasm, and in that chasm is no place for any man.
Johnny Cash

"When you leave home, we're breaking your plate."

My father always said those words with a wry smile, but I knew what he meant. He didn't want me to move back in after college—he expected me to do my best to make it on my own and live as independently as I could.

Now that Geoff had come home after his sophomore year, Dad's words kept coming back to me. I couldn't stop thinking about my own son's future and how difficult his life would be if he couldn't shake his addiction.

At least now he was making an effort. The rift with his sister after the incident in Wilmington had jarred him closer to reality. Geoff agreed to go back and talk to Gary, the outpatient rehab counselor who had been helpful for him in the past. He also took on work with a painting contractor in Durham. But he continued to struggle with his addiction and tried to hide it from us.

It's often said among families with an addicted loved one that "love must be tough." But what does that mean? Usually, the definition is one-sided. Tough love means enforcing consequences on someone's misbehavior. That's a necessary response to addiction, as far as it goes. But in our experience with Geoff, we found that it didn't go far enough because of the stress we were under and our own human selfishness and fallibility. We needed God to strengthen us and help us love our son beyond our natural ability.

Both my head and heart would hurt at times when we sat among families sharing their stories in recovery groups we visited. The greatest caution was taken not to enable a loved one's addictive behavior (that is, not doing something that would make it easier for their loved one to get their drug of choice, or allowing them to remain in a situation where they didn't face the consequences of their actions). But how could we be sure we were making the wisest choices and not being selfish ourselves?

When would it be the right decision to close the doors of our home to Geoff because of his addiction? Was that simply determined by our comfort zones and the degree to which we wanted to be inconvenienced? How could we know when the line had been crossed and truly ascertain what was best for our son? After all, "The heart is deceitful above all things and beyond cure. Who can understand it?" (Jeremiah 17:9). The conundrum drove us to prayer, and the more we prayed, the more we encountered the truth that real love—love like the kind Jesus demonstrated—also had to be tough on ourselves. Tougher than we sometimes wanted it to be.

We knew that God would have us demonstrate His sacrificial love to our son, and that meant we sometimes had to do things we really didn't want to do. We didn't like where our life was at the moment or the choices our son had made, but God continued to impress upon us that it would be a sin to walk away from Geoff in his time of need. Even though he had made the choices that had brought him into such difficulty, our love had to be "patient" and "kind," "not self-seeking," "not easily angered," not dwelling on Geoff's wrongs (1 Corinthians 13:4–5). That meant it would cost us time and money, and it would also draw us out of our individual comfort zones.

Sometimes Cari and I would have tension between us as a couple as we wrestled with trying to make the right choices for our son. Sometimes it felt like one or the other of us was putting our relationship with our son ahead of our relationship with one another. This happened because we both had different tolerances and opinions, and like any addict, Geoff would use this to his personal advantage. The end result was that he would play us against each other. He knew which of us to ask for whatever he was after.

God used this to stretch both of us, teaching us to communicate better with Him and with each other. We learned to be more intentional with our own relationship, taking time for each other when we could reasonably do so—even if it was just for a quick dinner out. Through all of this, God toughened our love for each other as well as for our son.

It was clear that God wouldn't want us to have Geoff continue to live in our home if he might be a danger to us. We also knew that he couldn't stay if he continued to use drugs while showing no intention of getting better. But how do you measure someone's intentions when he is struggling with such a powerful addiction? Sometimes relapses would occur immediately after a day when there had been a positive step forward, and that was as devastating for Geoff as it was for us.

Little by little, God was helping us take a step back and see our son through a larger lens than his addiction. His addiction didn't define him—he was so much more than that! Just as God had loved us with an incarnational love, coming into this dark world and bending to us through the cross to save us, our own love for our son had to be incarnational, fleshed out in the most practical, everyday ways. Regardless of the darkness that surrounded him, Geoff needed us to walk with him through the dark and lead him into the light.

The daily struggle continued as his addiction took deeper, more desperate bites out of his body and soul. Spoons sometimes disappeared at home. We didn't notice they were missing at first. But we did notice that Geoff had fewer video games and had sold his Xbox console. "I'm saving up for the next one to come out," he told us. "They gave me credit at the store." One afternoon Geoff asked Cari if he could borrow $20 to go to the mall. He came back a couple of hours later, and she noticed a small red mark on his arm.

"It's a mosquito bite, Mom," he told her. But late one evening a few days later she found a hypodermic needle when she was washing his clothes. Then we found, under the bed in his room, a spoon with burn marks. We realized that Geoff had completely relapsed and was injecting heroin again.

We confronted him with it immediately, and even though he denied it at first, the next day he admitted that he had slid back into abuse. On the advice of another counselor, he decided to try a new approach to getting clean. He would enter a medically supervised, outpatient therapy program, considered to be cutting edge at the time.

The program used a synthetic opioid analgesic specifically designed to treat heroin dependency. The theory is that with proper monitoring, it can reduce the painful side effects of withdrawal and gradually allow the patient to quit altogether. Withdrawals are also less severe than with methadone.

Geoff did well on the program for a few months, but after a while he started to slip back into old ways. He began to be more secretive, opening up less about where he was going and what he was doing. There was a harder, cynical edge to his normally positive and upbeat personality. He smiled less, angered quickly, and rarely laughed at all. We were worried. One day we checked his cell phone when he was sleeping, and we found that he had been selling his prescribed dosage for the drugs he really wanted.

Cari had had enough. "He can't stay here. Not like this. I want him out of here today."

"Wait," I told her. I had begun to learn that reacting in the moment rarely got us where we needed to be. "Let's pray and see if there's another way out of this."

Usually, I had been the one to insist on a harder line with Geoff, but this time the tables were turned. It wasn't the first time we had tension between us because of Geoff's choices, and it was a difficult place to be. But this time I felt like Cari was making the same mistake I had made in the past, reacting in anger. We needed to wait things out for a week.

One morning several days later, I discovered that I had accidently left the safe where I kept his medication unlocked, and Geoff had helped himself to several packets. I knew he intended to sell them, so I confronted him.

"I didn't take them, Dad," he insisted.

Addicts can be so convincing, so accustomed to lying that they even persuade themselves to believe their own untruths. But I wasn't buying it.

"I know how many I counted, Geoff. There are five doses missing."

We were standing by the front door, and I stepped outside with him to the front porch to make the next point. "You know that your mom has been saying you need to leave, right? And it's usually never that way—and that should tell you something. I'm usually the one who insists on more drastic measures—so if I agree with her on this, there's nothing standing in the way. As hard as that is, you will have to leave. I don't want that, son. Please. You have until 4:00 p.m. today to come clean about the missing meds and to return them, or you're out."

Geoff held firm: "I didn't take them, Dad."

But a little over an hour later his demeanor had changed, and he returned the medication.

When I later told Cari what had happened, she responded, "What's it going to take to have him come around? He's hardly himself any more. This can't be his future."

"Maybe if we get him back to talk with Gary one more time," I responded.

"Gary deals with kids who are younger than Geoff, and our insurance won't keep covering that," Cari said. "But I know he will still make time for him. Geoff listens to him."

"Whatever it takes," I responded. "We need to do whatever we can to help him beat this."

The words surprised me as soon as they left my mouth. I realized that my heart was softening toward my son, regardless of what he had done. God was doing His own work over time, removing some of my harsher attitudes. I had begun to see how in spite of his addiction, Geoff and I were not that different. I had been wrestling with other things—especially anger and pride—but I was finally beginning to see how much grace and forgiveness both of us needed just to get through the day.

Gary did make time for Geoff, and after meeting with him one afternoon Geoff came home with a revelation.

"Dad, Mom . . . I want to get off of substances all together. No synthetic opiate therapy, nothing like that. There's a place Gary recommends where I can give that a try—some really good things have happened there. It's a rehab center in Tennessee that Johnny Cash went to—it's in Nashville. They have a bed available, and I want to go as soon as I can. Gary says our insurance will cover a lot of it. I'll be there over my birthday, but I don't care. I really want to do this."

Cari and I looked at each other and smiled. She was fighting back tears. "That's amazing!" she said.

In the days that followed, Geoff didn't waver. He was true to his word, and he left within the week.

One evening not long afterwards, Cari and I were at a fund-raising dinner for a local faith-based charity when we caught the eye of a distinguished-looking gentleman standing near us. We recognized him immediately. It was the judge Geoffrey had stood before a few years ago, when he had been in high school. The judge had a reputation for being tough but was also fair-minded.

"How's your son doing?" he asked us, with a glance that felt more searching than it was probably meant to be. Just seeing him again made me overly self-conscious and a little defensive.

I fumbled for words. "Well, there are some bright spots, but Geoff's still struggling. He's in rehab right now in Tennessee, but we're hopeful."

What happened next surprised me. A kind and knowing smile slowly crept up the judge's face, and he looked at us even more directly: "He'll have a story to tell one day. Right now he's just working on his testimony."

GEOFF

Desperation is the raw material of drastic change.
Only those who can leave behind everything they
have ever believed in can hope to escape.
WILLIAM S. BURROUGHS, THE NAKED LUNCH

"It doesn't look like the pictures," I muttered to myself as we drove under the archway that marked the entrance to the treatment center in Nashville. "There were pictures of horses, but I don't see any horses," I joked under my breath. Immediately after those words left my mouth I thought, "I am gonna need more than a horse to fix my issues." I have always had a cynical mind even in seemingly hope-filled situations.

After I checked in and said goodbye (what had by now become the usual routine), the nurses gave me a quick check-up. I wasn't going through withdrawals yet because of the pills I took just before arriving, but I still had to stay in the detox unit for the next week. They removed my phone and my iPod, and they put me on what they called blackout restriction. That meant no calls, TV, or any access to the outside world until my detox was over. I sat down on the side porch of the building and lit a cigarette, joining a large group of other patients in their first week of treatment.

Cigarettes seemed to be the cornerstone of community there. It was the only comfort we had with little to do, so we sucked down packs of cigarettes as fast as we could buy them. That day I struck up a conversation with a guy named Ryan. We had similar tastes in music, were both detoxing from heroin, and had some common experiences in life. In just a short time we became fast friends.

Time in treatment tends to pass extremely slowly. A month can feel like a whole year, and life outside trudges forward without your knowledge. This can prove to be mentally taxing, and it left me anxious and ready to go home. The first week is the easiest because you still have the crutch of detox medications like buprenorphine and valium. I never needed the valium, but I always lied about having a hefty addiction to alcohol, so they would prescribe it anyway. It was some sort of last hurrah (I suppose), but at the end of the day the detox medications were nothing in the face of heroin withdrawal.

After the first week passes and they taper you off of most medications, things start to become more difficult. I became incredibly sick and almost never slept, spending all day switching between being freezing cold and extremely hot. I was always sweating, and whatever food I managed to choke down would immediately come back up. Then in the evening my legs became so restless that staying in bed was a hopeless effort. My skin began to crawl, and I became delirious and unable to interact with the world around me. There are no words that can fully describe the horror of withdrawal from opiates. Even when I could stand the physical aspects, mental angst would take over. I would pace up and down the halls all night until I became bored, and I would head outside to walk around the campus.

One evening I found myself wandering about in a terrible mental state. I was riddled with anxiety and dread and was willing to do anything to put a stop to how I was feeling. I felt cornered. I knew I couldn't continue on as I was, but I also knew that the only thing that would make it stop was the very thing that would kill me: heroin. This led me to the conclusion that there was only one way out.

Death.

I was clutching a book of Bible verses my parents had given me on Easter one year as a last-ditch effort to get me to read Scripture. As the birds began to chirp—signaling the arrival of morning—I stumbled into a small chapel on campus where we had our morning meditations. I had been closed off to Scripture and God for a quite a while in my addiction, but that night I was grasping at anything—even what I thought were straws. I opened the book and flipped through it until I found a section titled Verses for When You're Suffering. If nothing else in this book was true, I knew this was. I was more than suffering. My eyes scanned the page until they rested on a verse in the middle of the page:

> When you pass through the waters,
>   I will be with you;
> and when you pass through the rivers,
>   they will not sweep over you.
> When you walk through the fire,
>   you will not be burned;
> the flames will not set you ablaze. (Isaiah 43:2)

Somehow as I read the words, sweet relief flooded my body. My anxiety melted away and my mind was calmed. I could not remember the last time I felt so at peace. I had been convinced that the Bible wasn't going to help me, and I also wasn't sure what I believed about God anymore. But in that moment something changed.

God stopped being this far off, negligent being who couldn't care less about what happened on earth and definitely did not care what happened to me. All of a sudden, He became personal to me. He became present in my life. He actually cared—deeply—about what happened to me. As time would pass I came to realize it wasn't His posture that changed but mine. I began to understand that God had been right there with me all along. He hadn't abandoned me. He hadn't forgotten about me. He didn't think I was trash. Rather He thought I was valuable enough to stand next to me in my mess every step of the way. When I read that verse, it was like God was speaking over me, "I am here. I have never left, and I never will—even when you do terrible things or curse my name."

While my physical withdrawal was still present, my mental state had changed. God was not going to take my suffering away. He was not going to instantaneously fix all my problems. I still had consequences for my actions and had to walk through those fires, but now there was another there with me.

That evening renewed my resolve. I knew I could get through this season and that I would come out on the other side alive. The rest of my treatment proved to be formative and helpful in my recovery. I came to realize how much of my physical struggle was controlled by my mind. If I focused on my symptoms, they were overwhelming. But when I filled my mind with other things, they were hardly even there.

During my stay in Nashville, God continued to put people in my life to speak truth to me. Some were not Christians, but they were people I could relate to. They would point me to my faith, not because they thought it was true, but because they knew I needed something bigger than myself to overcome my addiction.

As time went on, I became serious about my recovery. I had built trusting relationships with the counselors there, and they helped me grow in leaps and bounds. I learned how addiction affects the chemicals in your brain, and the callousness that surrounded my heart slowly began to fall away. Even back then, in the very beginning of my walk with God, He began to prepare me for what was to come.

I will never forget one of my counselors, Eric, calling me over after a particularly difficult group session. I was tired and frustrated and had gotten into it with another group member. He sat me down, looked me in the eyes, and told me, "You have this gift, Geoff, that not a lot of people have. When I walk in a room, I have to work to make people listen to me, respect me, and like me. It doesn't come easily for me, but you will never have to worry about that. You have that thing that lights up a room when you walk in the door. People instantly like and respect you. You can use it for great things or terrible things. But never forget it."

I had trouble believing his words and could not see what he saw. I felt like a loser, but I was learning how wrong that evaluation was. So many things happened during that treatment that would come to bear later in my life, and those thirty days were exceptionally formative.

Ryan and I had grown to be like brothers. We would stay up late into the night playing dominos and having deep conversations about life, God, and our intentions moving forward. If there were ever two people who were positive they would stay sober and make progress, it was us. We never wanted to return to the lifestyle we had so narrowly escaped and our community believed we wouldn't. What I did not know then, is that often it is the people who appear to have it all figured out that can fall the hardest.

Sometimes I wish that this were the end of my story. That I went to treatment, had a spiritual awakening, discovered God's purposes for my life, and never looked back. But it is rare that success comes so easily. It is rare that we do not glance back over our shoulder at our city of sin and meet our fate because of it. That would be a beautiful story—but it was not mine.

After completing our thirty-day stay, Ryan and I both moved into a recovery house in Nashville. A few other guys from the treatment center moved into the same one, and we had a strong community for the first few months. We found jobs, made friends, and began to build a life for ourselves. However, as time went on, our community began to shrink. Friends would relapse and leave, or they would get in a fight and get kicked out. After a while we became bored with a normal lifestyle. We were all used to chaos in our lives, and sometimes we would self-create it without even realizing it. We had found a church to attend and would go occasionally, but our pink cloud had begun to fade.

We were no longer desperate. Our lives were back together, we had gained weight back, our probation officers were happy. Things were no longer falling apart, and for a time that seemed really great. Eventually, though, we stopped being as diligent in our recovery. Neither of us realized it, but things were about to change. We put so much stock in our clean time and in ourselves that we forgot about what and who had ultimately changed our lives. God had taken a back seat in our lives, and we were both about to lose things that were precious to us. One of us would lose his clean time, and the other would lose his life.

8

In the Shadow

James

The prize is Jesus, God himself. The battle is worth it.
Edward T. Welch

"If you loved us enough, you'd quit."

Fair or not, that's how the families of many addicts often feel. When Geoff's drug abuse was ravaging his life and the lives of those closest to him, I expressed the same thoughts to him.

It had no effect. What we didn't understand was that the areas of his brain assailed by his drug habit were so primal that they temporarily hijacked areas that affected his thinking and feeling in relationships. This explains why so many addicts will continue in their substance abuse even at devastating cost to themselves and those they love.

Does this mean addicts don't bear responsibility for their behavior? No. But the chemical nature of addiction and its far-reaching effects on behavior also need to be taken into account. The sad thing is that while addicts have to take responsibility for their decisions because they chose to use in the first place, the consequence of the destruction of their relationships is often unintentional.

Geoff had been in rehab at the treatment center in Nashville for a few weeks. He had detoxed under medical supervision, and we were visiting for a parents' week. During those days Cari and I heard a lecture on the effects of opiate addiction on brain chemistry, and I immediately felt as if a weight had been lifted. I had taken so many of Geoff's choices personally, and I had felt so futile and powerless to make any difference in his life. I felt responsible somehow, and condemning thoughts had haunted me for some time, thoughts like, "If I had been a better dad, he never would have started to begin with." Or, "If I had just been closer to him, I would have been able to help him quit."

Slowly, things were beginning to be placed in perspective. One evening while in a group discussion with other families and their addicted loved ones, I looked around the room. As we sat and listened, I realized that most of the parents there felt as I did. Addiction had left the ugly, twisted wreckage of broken relationships in the lives of family after family. But there was still hope.

We were beginning to heal as a family. Now that Geoff had been away from illicit substances for a few weeks, he seemed more himself than we had seen him in a long time. He was beginning to take responsibility for his actions, and he openly asked forgiveness for the wrongs he had done. I had softened as well, and I was beginning to judge Geoff and our past less harshly. We still had a long way to go, but the sun was beginning to make its way out from behind the clouds.

There were still plenty of hurdles ahead of us. There were financial burdens and the resentment they caused. There were worries about whether the cycle of rehab and relapse we had seen in the past would repeat itself yet again (it would). But things were slowly beginning to change. God was doing a deeper work in all of us.

It helped to hear Geoff apologize and begin to take responsibility for choices he had made. It helped even more to hear his gratitude for the way we had continued to love him and walk with him through his struggle with addiction—not only because his gratitude made us feel good but also because it allowed us to see how God had held us up and loved him through us.

Still, the decision to forgive is one of the most challenging we face. Even though Jesus taught us to pray, "Forgive us our sins, for we also forgive everyone who sins against us" (Luke 11:4), we sometimes overlook the real meaning of those words. Behind them is the assumption that we will forgive, and if you take it a little further, there's an implied connection between our forgiving others and our being forgiven ourselves.

That's where it gets hard. We can't pray, "God, I want you to forgive me just like I forgive others" and truly mean it if we're really honest about how we personally struggle with forgiveness. But I can pray it and mean it if I let God love and forgive through me. Forgiveness becomes both an act of the will and a gift by which I humble myself before God and say, "I choose to forgive, but I can't do it in my own strength. I need your help, Lord Jesus! I need you to work it in me." And the One who cried from the cross "Father, forgive them, for they do not know what they are doing" (Luke 23:34) is faithful to give the gift and help us with something we could never accomplish on our own.

It certainly makes it easier when someone apologizes, but nowhere does Scripture say that our forgiving others should be dependent upon it. How often have we heard someone say, "I'll only forgive someone if they say they are sorry!" But Jesus doesn't teach us to forgive that way, as His cry of forgiveness from the cross makes clear.

This is a vital truth to grasp when someone you love is a prodigal and has made choices that have hurt you deeply. It may take years for them to understand the hurts they have caused, and they may never see them fully. But do any of us ever realize the full extent of our actions on others?

Today I look back on some things I did years ago and shake my head—and I know I still have my blind spots. Forgiveness is a precious gift. It is the working of God's grace within us. And where there is a struggle with addiction, forgiveness is needed constantly. Promises are made and broken. Old wounds are torn open just when we thought they had healed. In our own strength, it's impossible terrain. But God's grace "is sufficient," and his power "is made perfect in weakness" (2 Corinthians 12:9). As we come to understand how much we have been forgiven by God, we find ourselves asking for His help to forgive others with willing hearts.

Geoff would continue to do well for nearly a year after his initial visit to the treatment center in Nashville. He stayed in that city afterward because of the support he had in his recovery there. He moved into a halfway house, found a job, and rented an apartment on his own. He tried his best to surround himself with like-minded friends, and he would succeed for a while. But over time he would slip again.

Somewhere on the path of Geoff's struggle with addiction, someone had told us that when you begin with opiates as young as he did, the chances of recovery are slim to none. We didn't want to accept that, so we kept praying. We knew there was something huge missing from Geoff's recovery up to this point. After all he had been through, he still had not returned to God. There was talk of God. He believed in Him and asked for God's help with his sobriety, but it was a distant relationship at best.

It wasn't easy for him to find a faith community that would accept him with his struggle. He faced the same challenge we did as his parents. Could we openly share with others what we were really going through? Could we face that risk and have them accept us without judging us? Still, we were able to run to God and tell Him everything. As we walked through difficult places, He met us time and again. But Geoffrey wasn't there yet.

The giant he was facing with addiction was huge, and we had already seen it take the lives of several of his friends. The death of one young man hit us hard. Ryan was one of Geoff's close friends at the treatment center. I had spent time alone with him and Geoff during our visits, and I was surprised to discover that he was a very sincere believer. I longed for his faith to have an effect on Geoff and prayed that it would.

After he left the treatment center in Nashville, Ryan went to a halfway house where he was able to stay for a few months. He was eventually kicked out for a small, non-drug-related infraction (he came home later than he should have one night). Ryan started to use again out of frustration and discouragement, overdosed, and died.

That was the last thing any of us expected to happen. We had been so hopeful that Ryan was going to make it—he had so many things in his favor. He was young, intelligent, and outgoing. He had sincere faith and a supportive family. "Why hadn't God intervened somehow?" I wondered. The reality of the dangers our own son faced hit with full force. And the realization that Geoff was trying to navigate those waters without God hit harder still. Opiate abuse had become a national epidemic, and Shakespeare's poignant and memorable words captured the moment: "Each new day new widows howl, new orphans cry, new sorrows strike heaven on the face."

We chose to believe that heaven wept with us. And though questions remained, the gravity drove us to our knees again. I kept on praying and crying out to God, longing for Him to intervene in a tangible way. I prayed for Geoff. I prayed for Ryan's family and for wisdom to face the challenges ahead. We didn't know why

God had allowed Ryan to be taken so young, but we had already seen God's footprints on this hard, long road. We resolved to keep praying and to stand in the shadow of the giant with faith, believing that God was larger still.

Geoff seemed to be in a holding pattern. He'd do well for a while and relapse again. He would hold down one job and then have to leave it. He'd visit home and his eyes would be clear and his glance direct, but then, months later, we could tell just from the sound of his voice over the phone that he was struggling again. But he was sober for his twenty-first birthday, and that was a milestone to celebrate.

It was during those days that Cari said something that surprised me. One night we were talking quietly about how to best help Geoff out of another mess when the expression on her face turned thoughtful.

"What is it?" I asked her.

"You might think this is crazy," she said. "But the other day when I was praying for Geoff, I started thinking that God is going to use Geoffrey in ministry someday. And the thought won't go away. I believe that everything he's gone through can be used for good."

I nodded my head and managed a smile, but I didn't say anything. I couldn't get there from where we were.

But God could. Sometimes when we pray, God gives us gifts that are just for us, something to strengthen and encourage us that is a direct result of our time in His presence. In that moment God had shown Cari something that wouldn't happen for years. But happen it would.

We just had to follow Him there.

GEOFF

This is the way the world ends,
Not with a bang but a whimper.
T. S. ELIOT, "THE HOLLOW MEN"

Living in a halfway house is one of the more difficult things I experienced in recovery. You are made to walk the line between being institutionalized and having a normal life. You may feel like you are ready to move into your own home, but you have to continually remind yourself that you need accountability and safeguards in place. You get to be a part of society again, get a job, go to school, make friends, do different activities on the weekend.

When you are not at home, you have a normal life. However, when you get home, that changes: You have to sign in and out, be home by a certain time, take drug tests, and have people check in on you. With that sort of living situation comes a lot of shame when you are around people who aren't from the recovery world. You don't want to tell coworkers or friends you're in a halfway house. You would love to have them over, and you want to live what most see as a normal life. Moreover, you feel like you are capable of doing that, but the reality is that you probably are not there yet. In this process I learned that what I thought was my alter ego wanted me dead, told me lies, and convinced me that I was totally fine. Looking back, I know that it was the Enemy who planted those thoughts.

It was incredibly difficult for me in Nashville after leaving treatment. I made friends, got a job, and began to do all of the things that you want to see from a person in recovery. It seemed that every good thing I gained fed into a lie I was chasing—the lie that if I could just have the next thing, I would be normal. That was always a weak point when it came to my recovery. I wanted so badly just to be what I thought was normal from the world's point of view. I didn't want to identify as an addict. I didn't want to not be able to drink one beer. I didn't want to have to constantly monitor and think about my sobriety. I had no idea that the Lord's strength was made perfect in weakness, so I desperately wanted to cover my weaknesses up.

When I met a girl at work named Anna and we began to grow closer, I didn't immediately tell her about my life. I acted like I was the normal person I longed to be. One night after work, she was having our coworkers over to hang out. They were all having a beer, and I decided to have one too. *Just one beer with friends*, I told myself. No big deal. Not going to get drunk, not going to do drugs, just going to have fun with friends like normal people do.

I was able to keep up appearances for a while. I had one beer every now and again for a few months, and by the time I disclosed my past to Anna, she too thought it was totally normal for me to do that. She did not have much previous experience with people in recovery, but she was incredible about supporting me in my sobriety. At first, I didn't realize I was being deceived and did not understand what was happening. I didn't comprehend where this road would take me, and I genuinely thought I could continue to live as I was living.

It was as if my eyes were veiled to the truth, and I couldn't see the freight train called relapse approaching at breakneck speed. Steadily, my addiction returned. It started with smoking weed again, then a pill here and there. Eventually I was back on heroin. I had convinced Anna that everything was fine. Without her realizing it, I had manipulated our relationship.

After Ryan died, I was in a dark place, and Anna was there for me as I was struggling with grief. But I used his death as a reason for my relapse, and her empathy kept her right where I wanted her. It's amazing how we can eventually convince ourselves of our own lies. I truly believed that I was okay and not that bad off. I really believed that I had to do the things I was doing. I desperately wanted to stay away from opiates, but I also did not want to feel so much despair. The emotion was just too much to bear, and when I looked at what I thought was the only alternative to addiction, I didn't want it.

As wonderful as some recovery communities can be, a lot of groups tend to think they hold the exclusive answer to all the problems of addiction. They imply that if you just stick with it you can make it. It almost feels like a pyramid scheme: if you don't succeed in your goals, it's your fault alone. Some urge you to find a higher power, but at the same time they slander anyone who puts what they see as too much value in any spiritual pursuits. This kind of thinking persuaded me that God wasn't the answer and that Jesus really wouldn't help me.

The only thing that would help me was working the program and doing what I was told. I had seen that work for countless others, and I wanted it to work for me. However, when I met people with vast amounts of clean time, it scared me. I did not want to be what they were. Some seemed so miserable, and they all seemed to have a chip on their shoulder. They were militant about their method of recovery, and that just seemed like another addiction to me. I was told I would have to do certain things for the rest of my life and that if I didn't, I would be right back where I was.

While I did not want my previous lifestyle, I also didn't want the new one that recovery seemed to offer me—so I left it. I already knew the story I was entering into because I had done it so many times before: be light and easy on the drugs for a few months before giving up and diving veins-first into a pile of heroin.

By the time I did that, Anna was at a loss for what to do. I used her grace and love against her, and I manipulated her into sticking around in a relationship that was emotionally abusive and wholly unhealthy. I began to steal money from her—and whatever else I thought I needed. She caught me multiple times and knew what was going on, but I would apologize profusely and promise her that I would never do it again. She would forgive me and take me back, trusting me and believing that I was going to turn it around. Unfortunately, that didn't happen.

My addiction grew larger than it ever was before, and I began to live a lifestyle that was exceedingly dangerous. I had never lived in such a big city before, and the drugs flowed much more freely in Nashville. I couldn't keep a normal job, but I did what I needed to do for my addiction. I sold drugs, robbed people, acted as a gun-toting guard for larger drug deals. I did whatever I had to do to get my daily fix.

Many times, I would find myself waking up in a random parking lot in East Nashville with a needle in my arm and a gun under my seat. I would shake off my high, start the car, and drive back home. No big deal. Time and time again I overdosed or people around me did. My first inclination was always to rifle through their pockets, take what money or drugs they had, and then push them out of the car. They did the same to me, and we would not even get mad about it. We all knew the lifestyle we signed up for and all the perks that came with it. You couldn't blame each other because you would do the exact same thing. This was the community I had chosen and the people I surrounded myself with. This was the normal I had found.

One morning, as usual, I woke up in withdrawal and got ready to go find my fix. My car had broken down a few weeks before, and I no longer had my license. Anna was totally over my lifestyle and would no longer let me drive her car, but that morning she was asleep. I slid out of bed, grabbed her keys, and pulled her debit card out of her wallet. I snuck out of the house, went by the ATM, withdrew money, and headed to my dealer's house.

After securing my fix for the day, I began to drive home in an attempt to get there before Anna woke up. Halfway there, I became so sick I couldn't drive, so I decided to do my shot right there. I pulled over to the side of the road, loaded up my syringe with all the heroin I had, put the needle in my arm, and pressed down the plunger. I quickly put the car back in drive, and I sped up to about fifty miles per hour. Just as I reached that speed, that familiar feeling of bliss overtook me. At first it felt so good—everything I thought I needed—until everything went black.

I remember only fragments of what happened next as I was fading in and out of consciousness. Opening my eyes and looking out the car window, I slid sideways toward a telephone pole. I felt the impact when I hit it, and I heard glass break. Soon someone was trying to pull me out of the car because I was completely out of it. I recall the ambulance arriving, the police showing up, and then waking up in a hospital bed.

I was beyond lucky to be alive. The police decided to charge me, and I dreaded what I had to do next: call Anna and then my parents to tell them what happened. I had stolen Anna's money, taken her car, overdosed behind the wheel, almost killed myself. Now I was headed back to jail, and my relationship with Anna was over.

This event ended up being a rock bottom place for me. It did not push me toward God or change my life forever, but I began to realize the depth of my sin. I knew that I would not continue living if something didn't change, so I began a slow trudge out of the darkness. I was still lost, still broken, still addicted, yet something was beginning to change.

I went to treatment as soon as I could. And once again, I achieved sobriety—only to turn my back on God again. But this time things seemed different. I was tired of addiction and the lifestyle that came with it. I finally saw it for what it was and knew that I didn't want to die. At long last I had proven to myself that there was no normal life for me that included substance abuse.

I began to rely on other things that would fill the Jesus-shaped hole in my life, and I soon entered into yet another relationship.

Relationships had become another escape from reality and addiction that I had to have, especially if I was going to be sober.

Heather and I had met in rehab, and neither of us were in a good place emotionally. After we had dated for several months, she came and told me she was pregnant with my child. I was excited but also nervous. I had recently gotten a steady job and was beginning to enjoy my life again and see my future in a new way. I broke the news to my parents, and although the situation wasn't ideal or in keeping with what they believed as evangelical Christians (they had both waited until they were married for an intimate relationship), they helped me prepare for my new life as a father. I thought this was the start of my growing into the life I always thought I would have one day.

Then everything turned. When Heather came to me and said she needed to tell me something important, I had no idea what was coming. She sat me down and explained to me that she had cheated on me, and the child wasn't mine. It hit me like a ton of bricks. The only two things that had kept me sober were that relationship and the child I thought I had. Losing both of those in a single moment was devastating. Amidst comments from friends that I had "dodged a bullet" and that "it wasn't such a bad thing," I turned to the only thing I had.

I had lost all control, and the last thing I could keep control of was my sobriety. So I threw it out the window. I didn't waste my time trying to control it or slowly delve back into it. I went straight back to heroin. I didn't lie to myself and try to be okay or put on a show for the people around me. Still, somehow I desperately wanted to end it. And after a few weeks, I was done.

I finally walked into treatment for what I knew would be the last time. My thinking was that if it didn't work this time, I would just end my life. I was so tired of living like I had. I was hurt and so was my family. I had zero hope and zero will to live. "It would be easier if I just died," I reasoned.

I did the usual detox and thought about my options: where I would go, what I would do, who I would be. I had been thinking that my life was set and that I would work a full-time job and have a family—something I had always wanted. But now that option was gone. Now I felt like my only other option was to be the miserable person in recovery, repeating the same program and lifestyle until I grew old and died. I didn't want that either.

As I slid into my inevitable detox stupor, I came to the decision that I didn't want what life had to offer. I didn't see any hope or anything I wanted, I didn't want the identity of an addict, and I didn't want to do programs or live in halfway houses. I didn't want to be in and out of jail. I didn't want to be some religious weirdo.

I had one choice.

One night at the treatment center I was so sick that I wanted to leave. My plan was to go get heroin and just get high until I overdosed and died, which shouldn't be hard with my low tolerance from detoxing. It was about midnight, and I approached the late-night nurses' desk. I choked out the words, "Give me my stuff. I am signing myself out and going home."

The lady behind the desk was nearing retirement, and I could see in her eyes that she had done this before. "What's wrong, sweetie? Why don't we talk about it before you go?" she asked, knowing what my leaving would lead to. She had seen me in treatment several times before, and she knew what happens when repeat patients leave at midnight. They die.

"I don't wanna talk about it. I just want to go, so give me my stuff," I shot back. I didn't have time to deal with this, and I was too emotional to have any sort of conversation about what was wrong with me.

"You know I can't just do that," she said. It felt like she knew exactly how I felt and exactly what I wanted to do.

"What do you mean you can't just do that?" I answered. "You have to do that! I am an adult and I signed myself in, I can leave when I want."

I was beginning to grow frustrated and almost wanted to yell.

"I will call the cops if I have to," I threatened. I didn't realize how ironic that must have seemed for someone who spoke so negatively of police to threaten to call them.

"Do whatever you feel like you need to do," she smiled back sweetly. "I am not giving you your keys!" She somehow managed to say it in the kindest, most loving tone I have ever heard.

I eventually broke down crying and sat down next to the nurses' station and poured out my heart to this lady. She hugged me and prayed for me and listened to all of my frustration and the pain that I felt stuck in.

I did not realize it at the time, but that nurse had put her job on the line that night. It was illegal for her to not let me leave, but she didn't care. I actually could have called the police and left—and she probably would have gotten fired. But she had held strong. Her decision to not let me leave saved my life that night. It wasn't until years later that I realized my parents had been up late that same night, kept awake by a perceived need to pray hard for me.

God was at work even though I didn't want Him to be. I fought against Him. I had glimpses of His mercy when I was at my lowest points, but I didn't trust that there was something really there. I pushed to go the other way. I fought to be something different. I wanted anything but Jesus. The last thing I wanted to be, as I saw it, was a goody two-shoes Christian who thumped the Bible at others and hated people who weren't like him.

I wouldn't give God a chance, but little by little He was chipping away at my heart. I thought about the time in rehab when I read Isaiah 43:2 and felt at peace. I thought about all the moments when I should have died but didn't. I thought about the grace and the love my parents had shown for me. I looked at everyone I knew who didn't make it and wondered how I had survived. There was something greater than myself at work, but I was blind to it. I thought I knew what it was to be a Christian, and I wanted nothing to do with it. But over time, even that would change. God was preparing me for something that I never expected and never wanted.

He was going to kill the old me.

9

"JESUS CAMP"

JAMES

Judge not the Lord by feeble sense, but trust Him for His
grace. Behind a frowning providence he hides a smiling face.
WILLIAM COWPER, "GOD MOVES IN MYSTERIOUS WAYS"

We were relieved whenever Geoff was able to break free of the grip of heroin and take steps into freedom. But there was still something missing, and it concerned us deeply because we knew he could never truly be free without it.

Geoff wasn't living in a relationship with Jesus. God may have been a means to an end—providing inspiration for his sobriety and mercifully meeting many of his needs, but the deepest thirsting of his soul had not been quenched with "living water"

(John 7:37–38). As long as that well was dry, the void within could cause him to crumble in on himself at any moment.

So we kept praying, and as we did we sometimes caught glimpses of God's fingerprints.

One evening Geoff was visiting New Orleans with friends during Mardi Gras. Cari and I were worried about the trip and tried to talk Geoff out of it—but he was an adult and already lived away from home, so our options were limited. While he was there, we felt moved to take the day to fast together and pray. When the phone rang that evening and Geoff's number came up on caller ID, our past experience conditioned us to think the worst. But Geoff's voice was strong and clear: "Dad, the coolest thing just happened. We were walking through the French Quarter and came to one corner where some religious people were holding up signs and pointing and shouting at us. We kept on walking. Then we got to the next corner when another group from a church came up to us. They were really nice. They welcomed us and asked if there was anything they could pray for us about. Then we prayed together right there on the street. It was pretty cool. I thought you might like to know."

When we hung up the phone, Cari and I looked at each other and laughed. Not only had the bad news we had expected not come but we also saw another example of how God hadn't given up on Geoff. No matter how far away our son may have been, we had just been shown yet again that he couldn't escape God's reach: "the arm of the LORD is not too short to save, nor his ear too dull to hear" (Isaiah 59:1). That moment was another reminder why our prayers mattered, and we were determined to pray all the more and to ask others to join us. Prayer offered us a way into Geoff's heart when so many other efforts had failed.

Ole Hallesby wrote, "Prayer and helplessness are inseparable. Only those who are helpless can truly pray."[7] We had a growing realization that although we could not change Geoff, God could. This drove us to be increasingly open in asking others to pray for us.

Early one morning I was in the car with my author friend Daniel Henderson and his sons on the way to the Brooklyn Tabernacle, where Daniel was holding a teaching event on prayer. One of the reasons I wanted to visit the Brooklyn Tabernacle was because of what had happened there. Jim Cymbala, the pastor, had faced his own struggles with a prodigal. One Tuesday night as the church interceded for his daughter at a prayer meeting, God intervened in a remarkable way that resulted in her returning to faith in Jesus.[8] I was inspired by the story and wanted to learn what I could to encourage us as we prayed.

It was a nine-hour drive, and as the miles rolled on I opened up to Daniel about Geoff and his substance abuse. He listened thoughtfully and then began to pray. Then one of his sons joined in, and we found ourselves praying for some time. In those hours before dawn I was reminded yet again of what a gift others' prayers can be. One of the most powerful and effective ways to love others is to pray for them, because through our prayers God's creative power and restoring love flows afresh into their lives and accomplishes what only He can do.

Geoff needed that power and love more than anything, but there were also seasons while we prayed for him when his life seemed to unravel all the more. We had seen this happen before when we had prayed hard for Geoff—sometimes the dark places got darker still. This did not mean that our prayers were not effective. God has ways of breaking through and affirming His presence even when answers do not seem to come.

"Criticism of prayer," P. T. Forsyth wrote, "dissolves in the experience of it. When the soul is at close quarters with God, it becomes enlarged enough to hold together in harmony things that oppose, and to have room for harmonious contraries."[9] What we couldn't see at the time was that the spiritual battle we were facing was at a tipping point and was about to turn. It was the hardest place we had ever been in—but that difficulty and heartbreak pressed us into new dependence on God.

Life had become intolerable for Geoff in Nashville. Even though he seemed to have longer stretches of sobriety, when he fell, he fell harder. His addiction was worsening, and he began to face legal consequences again. He had wrecked a girlfriend's car because of driving while high, he was unable to hold down a job, and he had run out of money. He then rebounded into a rocky relationship with a girl who struggled with substance abuse. After she deceived him into thinking she was pregnant with his baby, she left him for the baby's actual father and took out a restraining order when Geoff, heartbroken, began sending her text messages around the clock. He then relapsed and found himself in detox in a treatment center yet again.

Nashville had become just another spot on the map that was no longer working out, and Cari and I had had enough. But what was the next step? Where could he go from there? We were tired of simply changing locations and thinking that would somehow change him. Geoff was in trouble wherever he went, and a deeper change was needed. He was an adult and could make his own decisions, but because of his recent job loss and difficulties he found himself dependent on us again financially.

So we made it clear that we would no longer support his getting sober in Nashville. "This time," Cari told him, "you're going to do it our way. When you get out of detox, you'll need to go into a rehab living situation as soon as possible for an extended time. And if we're going to pay for it, it's going to be a place we choose for you—it needs to be faith-based."

Because Geoff had no other options, he reluctantly agreed. This alone was a victory. Along the way, God had shown us that the way forward with our son was to stay in communication with him and keep loving him regardless of the circumstances. We did our best to be there for him emotionally even when we withheld support financially. Conversations, no matter how difficult, continued to end with "I love you." After all, if we weren't there for Geoff when he hit rock bottom, who would be? We had seen too many wrecked lives among his friends who had been completely cut off.

As soon as Geoff was released from another detox episode—this time at a hospital—Cari and I made the nine-hour drive to Nashville on a rainy January morning in a U-Haul truck. Geoff was quiet and discouraged as we loaded up his belongings. Cari and I slept fitfully that night and were up early, wanting to put Nashville in the rearview mirror as quickly as possible.

The moment we were out of bed Geoff started in: "Dad, Mom, please. I want to stay. Isn't there another way? I have friends here. There's a good rehab community here. Don't make me leave."

We did our best to avoid the conversation and distract him with the details of moving. But an hour after we had pulled away, we stopped at a restaurant just outside the city limits. Geoff broke down and began to plead. "Mom, Dad, please! I won't mess up again. I promise. I can't leave here." His voice swelled with grief and the tears flowed. He couldn't help himself, and the people sitting around us were starting to notice.

We felt terrible. My heart was breaking for my son—it grieved me to see him so sad and desperate. Somehow this was even worse than seeing him behind the plexiglass at the jail. He was free, but so enslaved—and my heart went out to him. Cari and I knew we couldn't give in, but it still hurt to hold our resolve. Minutes crept by like hours. All I could do was pray in the moment, "God, please. Get us through this. Help him. Please, make a way." We left as soon as we could, and Geoff fell asleep in the truck. I breathed a sigh of relief and quietly wept while I drove.

We were all exhausted physically and emotionally.

But Cari and I had yet another glimmer of hope. She had found a promising faith-based recovery house in Wilmington, not too far from our home in Durham. Even though Geoff had tried and failed in Wilmington before, we were reaching for more than sobriety alone. "If only Geoff could catch a glimpse of God's love for him, if only he would let Jesus in . . ." We had this conversation many times, and we were laser-focused on doing our part to help Geoff make a new discovery of faith.

We had learned from experience that when Geoff detoxed from heroin he would need to enter a stable recovery environment as soon as possible. We returned the U-Haul truck early the next morning in Durham. By evening, we had packed his things and were on the way to Wilmington, where we all stayed at our daughter's home.

The next morning we had a family interview with Elizabeth at Christian Recovery Houses (CRH). I was immediately touched by her compassion for Geoff. She had struggled with substance abuse herself, and she was understanding with Geoff when he rebuffed her gentle questions with sullen responses. He did not want to be there, and he wasn't being subtle about it. As the interview concluded, Elizabeth did something that touched us both deeply. "Would you mind if we prayed?" she asked. As soon as she said it, I was assured we had found the place Geoff needed to be.

We had barely pulled out of the CRH parking lot when Geoff began to protest: "I'm not going to 'Jesus camp.'"

We said nothing. Then he started up again.

"This place isn't going to help me. I'm not going."

I was tired and my temper's fuse was short.

"Yes, you are!" I fired back. "That is if you want any help from us whatsoever."

"I don't care," Geoff answered. "I'll live on the street if I have to."

We were facing a spiritual battle with Geoff. The darkness that had held him so tightly in its talons would not release its grip without a fight. Geoff and I kept arguing, and even Cari entered into the fray. Scarcely three miles from our daughter's house I pulled into a McDonald's parking lot too upset to drive.

"Go ahead!" I shouted. "But if you don't go, know this. We're DONE. No help. No support. No cell phone. NOTHING."

"Think about that, Geoffrey," Cari added. "We mean this—we really mean it. And even though it will be hard, it's the only thing we can do. We've run out of options with you."

"FINE!" he shouted back. "But I'm not going."

Geoff meant what he said. When we arrived at the house, I had calmed down. But Cari and I both knew what his refusal to go would mean. He would be without a place to stay, and he would be out on the streets of Wilmington where he had abused heroin before. Even though my emotions were raw and I was still angry, I kept praying silently in desperation. Then . . . an idea.

I couldn't talk to Geoff—I was clearly getting nowhere. But Justin, our daughter's boyfriend, had just shown up and was hanging out that afternoon. He was an Iraq War veteran who had seen combat in difficult missions, and Geoff looked up to him. A few minutes after he arrived at the house, I pulled him aside and explained the situation.

"I can't get through to Geoff," I told him. "And I'm afraid he's going to kill himself if he doesn't go. But Geoff really respects you. Could you talk to him?"

"I'll do my best," he responded quietly. "But I can't promise anything."

A little later that afternoon he and Geoff went for a walk. When they returned, Geoff had agreed to go to CRH.

"What did you tell him?" I asked Justin later.

"I told him to just give it a try for a couple of months—you can do anything for that long. What do you have to lose?" Then he laughed and added, "That way he could say that he'd done it, and he'd get you off his back."

We took Geoff to CRH the next morning. We didn't know it yet, but the long, dark night was coming to an end. We were about to see the sun.

GEOFF

*Jesus' goal for his followers is never just a life without
obvious sin, but a life filled with genuine love.*
BRUXY CAVEY, THE END OF RELIGION

My mother had tears streaming down her face as Elizabeth prayed over our situation. She had met us at CRH an hour earlier to show us around the place. I still wasn't convinced it was where I needed to be, but I felt a pang of guilt as I watched my parents with my eyes still opened while Elizabeth prayed. Their brows were furrowed, eyes clenched shut, and they were begging God that this would be the last time my family would go through this. No more treatment centers, hospitals, jails, or wondering if I would die. They were done with it. I didn't know how much more they could take, and I was nearing the end as well.

I was exhausted and tired of constantly striving to fill an unquenchable need. Addiction is a full-time job, and you are never off the clock. People had told me that if I worked half as hard at bettering myself as I did at my addiction, anything in the world was within reach.

As Elizabeth wrapped up her heartfelt prayer, I realized that this was not her first time saying a prayer for a broken-hearted family member. At first, I thought it was a well-rehearsed sales tactic, but I would come to learn that she meant every word she spoke. It was clear that she had been there for many people like us—people who were at a loss for what to do and saw in CRH one last glimmer of hope.

She overflowed with empathy as she comforted my mother. It was strange to sit on the couch and hear my mother discuss the pain I had put my family through. As I listened to the description of some of my worst moments, it felt like we were talking about someone else. Not me—but some other person who did terrible things in my name.

Later that evening I listened to myself agree to enter the program there.

Almost immediately, I regretted it. Now I was committed. I had tried everything to convince my parents that this wasn't the place I should be. I didn't want to be any place that was going to try to cram God down my throat. I thought it was a waste of time and full of judgmental, stuffy people who could never relate to me. Not only that but it was also in Wilmington—the same town where I used to run around downtown and get high. How was I ever supposed to stay sober with that sort of temptation right down the street?

No matter how much I begged and made excuses, my parents were firm in their resolve. They had made up their mind that if they were going to help me out for the umpteenth time, then I was going to attend a Christian program. If I wanted to go somewhere else, then I would have to figure that out myself.

That evening I moved my things into the house, and I met my three new roommates. On first impression, they all struck me as a little off-kilter. They initially confirmed everything I said about this place, and I thought they were nothing like me. They were alcoholics, and I never cared that much for alcohol. They were firm in their beliefs, and I thought they were ignorant to reality. I noted a long list of reasons not to like them, and I kept that list close for my first few weeks in the house.

As I began to settle back into Wilmington, I slowly started to build a normal life. My parents' confidence in me was beginning to be restored, and they loaned me the family car to drive while I was in Wilmington. I had friends here from my college days, but they had changed quite a bit. In fact, they proved to be a godsend. They helped me find a job at a local retail store, and I could spend time with them when I needed to get away from CRH. They were incredibly supportive of my recovery and continually pushed me to be a better version of myself. I still hadn't made deep connections in the program I was in, but my old friends helped me warm up to the idea of being there.

CRH required its residents to attend a local church called Port City Community Church. I had never been in a large church before, and I had looked down on them most of my life. So when I went for the first few months, I did everything I could to make people who attended there hate me. I would find the most obnoxiously vulgar music I could and blast it as I pulled into the parking lot. I'd hop out of my car and put out my cigarette on the door before flicking the butt in the bushes. I was doing my best to confirm everything that I knew about judgmental, angry Christians—but to no avail. Nobody yelled at me or used a Bible verse as a weapon. They didn't cast angry glances my way or stare at the floor when I walked by. Instead, they greeted me with uncommon grace and love. I was not accustomed to Christians treating me this way, and I was at a loss for how to respond.

The Sunday experience wasn't anything I was used to either, for the loud music and large crowds were off-putting at first. Over time, I made acquaintances there, and the crowd began to feel much smaller. Slowly but surely, the people I had set out to make angry were becoming my friends.

The following season of my life was an emotional roller coaster. While I had begun to settle into the community, I still felt uneasy about being in Wilmington. I enjoyed going to church to see people, but I remained skeptical to the idea of any spiritual belief. I had so many questions, hang ups, and frustration with what I thought was just another religion. At the time, it seemed to me that the only thing that mattered in religion was rules and rituals—and I thought that if I didn't believe what the church people did, they would hate me.

I had seen too many people use anger to try to convince people to put their faith in an all-loving God. I didn't know that there was another side of Christianity with people who were authentic, kind, and loving. Eventually, I would come to see it. I needed someone to tell me why I should choose to follow a man who lived thousands of years ago and started a movement that, while responsible for many great things, had also been accused of some terrible things in history.

The other thing that held me back from my belief was that I had yet to meet people in the church who I thought were like me. I saw myself as a rebel who surfed, skated, and listened to punk rock and rap. I assumed that there wasn't room for people like me in the church. Why would people obsessed with rules want to be around someone who intentionally broke them?

If only I had been willing to read Scripture, I would have seen that I was not the only person in the church who pushed back against that kind of religion. There was Someone else who pushed back against rule followers and law keepers. The truth was that I was in good company. Coming to understand this reality would change my beliefs forever.

I would come to discover many other new things about Jesus. He was not the founder of a religion. He isn't the creator of a list of laws and rules to live by. In fact, He repeatedly made the hyper-religious people upset because of what He taught and how He lived. So much about Him—including the people He spent His time with—put on display that following Him isn't about saying the right things or not having tattoos. I discovered that it isn't about putting on your Sunday best and showing up for church. It was a revelation to find out that what it truly looks like to follow Him is to love God and love others (Matthew 22:36–40). What came into focus about Jesus was that He is the cornerstone of a new way of life that sets people free and changes the way we interact with God forever. While I was starting to come closer to seeing these things, I was somehow still very far away.

I had so many victories and great days during that time in Wilmington, but I still experienced weak moments—those moments when I was frustrated, anxious, and unsure. At times it took everything in me to white-knuckle through the rest of the day and not use drugs. Sometimes there were things that caused those moments—such as a person who didn't understand where I came from making a poorly timed joke about my lifestyle. Other times it felt like an attack from the Enemy.

One day during a particularly dark moment, I found myself at an edge. I was bored with recovery, bored with life, and lonely. I had found people I cared about but had yet to find a true, close friend who was going through the same things I was. I was longing for a real connection with someone who understood. Without having anything better to do, I jumped in my car to go for a drive. Before I knew it and without consciously thinking much about it, I was downtown in the old neighborhood where I used to buy heroin. I drove around telling myself that I just wanted to see if anyone I knew was there.

That day was the only time I have ever driven down that block and not seen a single soul outside. No people standing on the block waiting for a car full of customers or even people milling about outside. I am still unsure what would have happened that day if I had found an old friend. Maybe just a conversation, maybe something worse. But I know that nothing short of a miracle left the streets empty that day. After driving by a few times, I finally gave up and drove back home depressed and defeated.

That evening when I arrived at CRH, there was a new resident unpacking his things. He said, "What's up, man, my name is Daniel." He shook my hand as I walked up to the doorstep. "Good to meet ya, Daniel. Where are you from?" Our conversation took off from there. He was tall with slicked back hair, had a half sleeve of tattoos, and wasn't over the age of forty, which meant that I may actually be able to be his friend. Seeing someone moving in that I thought I could connect with was like a breath of fresh air. He was outgoing, talkative, and we connected instantaneously.

As we talked, I learned that he had a family in town, had a great job, and had still decided to move into CRH. That baffled me. "Why would you live here if you don't absolutely have to?" I asked, no longer sure I was talking to a sane person. He explained that after being in recovery, he had relapsed and needed the extra accountability for the time being. Hearing someone willingly put himself into a program was new to me.

Daniel and I quickly became friends. We spent a lot of time together going to movies, surfing, and staying up late having conversations about faith. I felt comfortable with him and was able to spill all my frustrations about the church, Jesus, and everything that came along with it. It was nothing he hadn't asked himself before, and he pointed me in the direction of different books, pastors, and Scripture that I never would have sought out myself.

Slowly but surely, a lot of my questions were answered. I learned that just because some self-righteous person yelled something at me when I was in my addiction didn't mean it was true. I also unlearned a lot of things that I thought I knew. I finally stopped looking at Jesus as a purveyor of religion and began to see that following Him was so much more than that. I realized that what Jesus taught was the opposite of religion. He didn't give more rules and rituals—a lot of times He broke them. He didn't hate people; He loved them. Somehow this was all news to me—even though my parents and others had demonstrated His love to me in the past. Sometimes those we love are too close for us to see clearly what they are really all about.

Somewhere in the days that followed, I decided to truly follow Christ.

It wasn't a light-bulb moment, and there was no burning bush. It was arduous, difficult, and frustrating. I didn't raise my hand during an altar call or say a memorized prayer to rededicate my life. I simply chose to follow Jesus in every moment. Little by little my life began to look more like His.

From the outside, I looked nothing like how I thought a Christian would look. When I went to church, I wore brightly colored, ripped skinny jeans, sported a lip ring, and dangled a cigarette out of my mouth. I still tried to satisfy myself with things that would never truly satisfy. I chased girls, longed for money, got in fights, and did many other things all while trying to pursue a relationship with Christ. I was a work in progress. My life wasn't what a lot of people thought it should look like, but Jesus was moving in it, and I was growing toward Him.

Before I knew it, I took a look back and noticed that it had been a substantial amount of time since I had wanted to use drugs. Not just since I actually had done them, but since I had even thought about doing them. It was like I had stopped thinking about them and stopped caring about them. I no longer had to white-knuckle my way through the day, and my brain didn't wander there when I had nothing else to do. That was another flat-out miracle to me.

I could not remember the last time I had gone without wanting something. Something to satisfy, to make me feel better, to change my state of mind. Something to make me cooler or different or give me an identity or to make me feel loved. It had been a year since I had even thought about myself as an addict.

I was finally at peace with those around me, and I wanted for nothing. When I took an inventory of what was different and tried to figure out what had changed, there was one thing that had made the difference. One thing that had renewed my mind, one thing that brought me peace, one thing that forever changed who I was, one thing that removed my appetite for drugs.

Jesus.

10

NEW CREATION

JAMES

The great things of life are bestowed only upon those
who pray. But we learn to pray best in suffering.
PETER WUST

We kept holding our breath. Geoff had gone to CRH reluctantly, and Cari and I had grown so accustomed to rehab efforts not working out that we had to fight to have faith that things finally would work out. In the past, there was always some reason for it not ending well: unreasonable house rules, a personality conflict with a supervisor, a roommate who was intolerable. None of the reasons were good, but there was little we could do to stop Geoff if he chose to leave.

As new worries came up, we would bring them to God again and again until He somehow met us with peace. We had lived so long in problem-solving mode with Geoff that worrying was our natural means of coping. Yet ever so slowly, God was helping us change our rhythm of living. Worry was soul-consuming. Jesus alone could restore our souls, and He was gradually bringing us into His peace—regardless of the outcome on any given day with Geoff.

It was also His peace that we longed for more than anything else in Geoff's life. Geoff was angry and hurting from the deception of his previous relationship. He was disillusioned about his future after his initial failed attempts at college, and he felt as if his life was going nowhere. His dreams had been destroyed, his self-image was shattered, and his sobriety was hanging by a thread. Jesus could help him with all of that—if only Geoff would reach for Him.

The first few weeks at CRH passed without an incident, which surprised us. Then, a little after a month had passed, Geoff mentioned that one of his housemates had been kicked out for failing a drug test. Geoff began to push back on some of the rules against one of the house managers.

For now, he was staying the course. But we had been down this road before with him and didn't know how long he would continue. So we redoubled our efforts to pray. One of our most frequent prayers during that time was that God would send a friend who would have a lasting, positive influence on Geoff. We had prayed that in years past and nothing seemed to happen—but this time, a few weeks later, Daniel showed up.

Daniel was about ten years older than Geoff, but they shared interests in surfing, skateboarding, and spearfishing. Daniel had also struggled with substance abuse, but God had used his experience to draw him to a vital faith in Jesus. Daniel also lived locally, and he and his wife frequently had Geoff in their home. He became the older brother Geoffrey never had.

This was something new. Geoff was being warmly welcomed into a community of believers who struggled with the same things he did but had discovered the unconditional love of God. They loved and accepted Geoff even when he tried to push them away. Their attitude was often expressed to him with the words, "Just come to Jesus, and we'll figure the rest out later."

Watching from the outside in, it was one of the most beautiful things I have ever seen. Geoff and I had been involved in a battle of wills for so long that it had become difficult for me to persuade him to do anything—let alone encourage him in his faith. I couldn't relate to his struggle with substances, so it was easier for him to discount my advice. But now he was face to face with others who had been down the same prodigal path and had found nothing but emptiness. But somewhere on the road home, they met the Friend of Sinners (Matthew 11:19). And they helped Geoff understand Him and draw near to Him in a life-transforming way.

Another new friend was Mark. Mark was a surfer as well, and soon Geoff found himself distracted by healthy activities and thinking more about how the waves were breaking than about getting high. Mark was also one of the pastors at Port City Church, and he oversaw the Refuge ministry on Tuesday nights.

Refuge was just that—a place where those who wrestled with addiction could find acceptance and hope. Mark had been an addict for years himself and had lost a brother and a sister to the consequences of substance abuse. Now, a decade later, his goal was to help others make a new beginning and find their identity in Jesus's love for them.

Mark helped Geoff see that his deepest identity was not that of an addict—through his newfound faith in Jesus, he had become a "new creation" (2 Corinthians 5:17). Gradually, Geoff began to envision a new future for himself—not as a broken person, but as someone who was uniquely able to help and encourage others who struggled in the same ways precisely because of where he had been.

God wastes nothing. He was making Geoffrey stronger in the broken places. Geoff loved to serve others, and things that had once been a temptation to him were falling away. As he became increasingly involved with the Refuge ministry, he was even able to help other addicts clean up their apartments and discard their drug paraphernalia without being tripped up.

A transformation was happening before our eyes. What we had prayed for and worked for so long was finally happening—our son was seeing things in a new way, rediscovering the truths we had tried to share with him and making them his own.

It was also a rediscovery for me. As a pastor, I've had a front-row seat to God's life-changing work many times, and it never gets old. But when you see it happening to someone so close to you—your very own child—it's absolutely breathtaking. Still, I had to ask myself, "Why couldn't Geoff receive these truths from us years before?"

God's timing and purposes in saving a soul are beyond our reach. But one of the lasting takeaways from Geoff's situation is what a friend of sinners Jesus actually is. Jesus was more at home with sinners than with righteous people—because the sinners were able to admit their need, and He had come to save them in the middle of their mess.

God was also doing a work in my own heart, reminding me of my own desperate need for grace and forgiveness by showing me how deeply He loved those who were so far from Him. Jesus had left the ninety-nine to go after the one (Matthew 18:12), and in the parable of the prodigal son, he emphasized going the distance yet again: "*But while he was still a long way off*, his father saw him, and was filled with compassion for him; he ran to his son" (Luke 15:20, emphasis added). God was stretching my own soul with a new love for those who were a long way off, and He was giving me a fresh understanding of His amazing ability to reach them. He was "able to do immeasurably more" than I could "ask or imagine" (Ephesians 3:20)—and He was doing it right before our eyes, in the heart and life of our only son.

One particular incident brought that home to both Cari and me. Geoff had been at CRH for just about five months and had come home to visit for a couple of days. When he arrived in Durham, we noticed that his shoes were wearing out. So we hopped in his car and drove downtown to help him find a new pair. About a mile from home Geoff pulled out his cell phone and connected it to the car stereo. "There's something I really want you to hear," he said. "This is so good."

Great, I thought to myself cynically. *Here it comes. Another rap song that I'm going to have a hard time not giving a critique of. That's all we need. Just another thing to cause distance between us.*

But it wasn't a song. It was a sermon—a sermon by another former heroin addict telling about the difference Jesus is able to make in our lives.

As we rode along listening to the sermon, I was sitting in the passenger seat and Cari was in the back seat. I glanced back at her and her eyes were filled with tears. The next moment, mine were as well.

Geoff kept on driving, unaware of the depth of emotion that passed between his mother and me. Both of us were quietly weeping with joy as we witnessed the change in our son. It had been gradual—over the months the residual effects of opiates had slowly loosened their grip on his body, mind, and emotions, one finger at a time. But it was more than just that. Someone was prying those fingers loose, and the death-grip had been broken. Geoff had been changed by the expulsive power of a new affection. The things he loved before were being pushed out of his heart and life by a new love. He clearly loved Jesus, and he had come to new life in Him.

It was just a short ride, but I got out of the car with a very different perspective than when I had climbed in. Before, I had wondered. But now, I knew.

Jesus had set my son free.

GEOFF

We know what we are, but not what we may be.
WILLIAM SHAKESPEARE, *HAMLET*

"My name is Geoff and I struggled with substance abuse," I said, introducing myself to a large room of people who were at various stages of addiction or who had recently left it behind. We were in the musty basement of another church downtown and the smell of coffee and cigarettes wafted through the air. Some people scoffed under their breath and others turned around to look at me as I began to speak.

I still attended a specific recovery program three times a week because we were required to as residents of CRH. I was no longer crazy about going, but I still learned positive things every time I was there. When you wanted to say something in that context, you would introduce yourself by saying, "My name is ____ and I am a ____." You would identify yourself as an addict, or alcoholic, or some other form of the two. When I introduced myself as someone who struggled (past tense) with substance abuse, some people were bothered. They either thought I was arrogant and soon to relapse or that I was in denial. To insinuate that you no longer struggled with your addiction was taboo in some groups.

The purpose of identifying yourself in that struggle is wholly positive. It helps you admit you have a problem, keeps you humble, and reminds you that you never have the struggle completely beat. It reminds you to continually strive to grow. But I had been an attendee of similar programs for years and had always struggled with the idea of calling myself an addict. Something about it didn't sit right with me, and it took a long time to figure out why.

Not only was I required to attend that recovery program three times a week, but I also attended another program on Tuesday nights called Refuge. Refuge was at Port City Community Church (PC3) and was different from anything I had ever experienced. Over the past year, I had become good friends with the director of Refuge, Mark, who was also a pastor at PC3. We had connected on surfing, which with a little help from both Mark and Daniel, had grown from an occasional hobby to an everyday habit and (maybe) a slight addiction . . . but in the best way possible, because it connected me with a new group of friends at the church who were genuinely following Jesus.

Refuge became a home for me. I loved being there, loved the people, and loved the discussions we had. It was a fairly large group of people who attended, and the format was new to me. We would sit down and hear a teaching from someone and then break up into smaller groups of people who got to know each other really well. It was in those groups that I was able to open up about my struggles, my frustrations, and what I was learning. Over time, I began to gain a more Christocentric view of my past addiction.

I had always been told that once you became an addict, you were an addict for the rest of your life. That was your identity. There was nothing you could do to get rid of your problem, and you simply had to learn to manage it. I had fully adopted that viewpoint and felt like I had to fight against anything to the contrary—but in Refuge I began to hear something different. I learned that on some level everyone struggled with something similar to addiction. It wasn't always expressed in the context of substance abuse, but it was still the same thing: sin. The difference was that the sin in my life had become dominating. It crushed out everything else that tried to take hold, and it became the focal point of how I lived. The sentiment that there was nothing you could do about it and that your problem would be there forever was absolutely true. There is nothing you or I can do about our sin problem, and in our broken state, it would remain forever. However, there is Someone who has pulled us from that broken place.

When Christ died on the cross, we were set free from the bondage of sin and death. When we choose to follow Him, we are made one with Him in His death and we are counted dead to sin (Romans 6:3). Not only are we made one with Him in His death, but we are also raised again into new life (Romans 6:8), which means that although we have a lifelong illness that we are powerless to defeat, we are given a new life and a new identity that is void of that illness. Here is how Paul explains it: "Therefore, if anyone is in Christ, the new creation has come: The old has gone, the new is here!" (2 Corinthians 5:17). While this is simple to understand and the effects are instantaneous, it can take a lifetime to live into.

When I began to encounter verse after verse that spelled this concept out, I realized why it didn't feel right to identify as an addict all those years. Did I have a life-dominating sin? Yes. Had I been addicted to drugs? Yes. Did it define who I was? Of course not. Even in that identity, we are so much more than our actions—people should never be defined by the things they do in their darkest moments. Regardless, the wonderful truth that we get to rest in is that once we are in Christ we don't exist in those identities anymore. We are new creations. The man who lived that lifestyle? He is dead. That doesn't mean that I am not responsible for his actions or that I am not predisposed to certain sins. I will always have a tendency to resurrect my previous identity and do things that I used to do, but that is not who I am.

My pastor, Mike Ashcraft, told me once, "If God created life, He alone gets to define it." When God defines us, He doesn't call me or anyone else an addict. When we are in Christ, He calls us perfect, holy, and blameless (Colossians 1:22). What a beautiful identity we are given in our new lives! That is the life we are called to live in, and God is the only one who can give it to us.

Mark, Daniel, Mike, and many others helped me come to realize these truths, and they forever changed me. Even my life and pursuits began to look differently. I had just completed my first year back in school, and while I was a little older than most of the students, I still blended in well and made friends. School was no longer a chore to me, and I began to love it like I did when I was a kid. I made the dean's list each semester and held a 4.0 average. I was invited to join the honor's program, and even when I took classes that didn't come easily (like Honor's Calculus), I learned to work hard and push through it.

Along with my newfound drive and ability came all sorts of dreams and aspirations. Just as I had previously been told, when I worked hard at it anything was in reach. I found the words of my rehab counselor Eric to be true. People liked me. Sometimes I felt like half of my grades were earned because the professor and I got along well.

After a while, I had my eyes set on law school. I reasoned that being a lawyer was primarily about charisma and arguing things, both of which I was adept at. But as I pressed on toward that goal, I also began to give of my time at PC3. I led a small group of fifth-grade boys and had a blast with them every Sunday. I never thought I would be allowed to work with children, but my church was willing to give me a chance. It quickly became my favorite time of the week. The kids were funny, smart, and occasionally out of control—but they were also able to have serious conversations when the time came.

At the end of their fifth-grade year, I was given the option to take on another group or move up with them to the middle school ministry. The choice came easily. I went with them into the middle school ministry (Tsunami) and quickly fell in love with all that was happening. The chaos and craziness made me feel right at home in the best ways imaginable. Brett (the ministry director) and I became good friends, and he gave me plenty of responsibilities and room to grow.

At this same time, I was still heavily involved in Refuge. Mark challenged me in many ways, and he was a great mentor for me. I learned to speak, teach, and care for volunteers. I was blind to it, but God was using Mark and Brett to prepare me for something I would never expect.

Before all of that had begun, my time at CRH was coming to an end. I had lived in the house at that point for nearly a year and had grown in leaps and bounds during my time there. Daniel had moved out about three months before me, and I began to grow antsy. My time there had matured me. I learned to stop complaining about every little thing and learned to roll with it. I learned to live with others well, take care of my space, and keep a schedule. I also discovered that is was possible to complete a sentence without expletives.

At the house we had been given chores to do on a weekly basis, and one week mine was mowing the lawn. I knew that both Chancy, who was the manager of the house, and Daniel thought of me as a city boy who didn't know his right from his left, so I decided to play into that assumption.

I pulled the lawn mower out of the shed before getting them both and explaining, "Dude, I've never mowed a lawn before. How do I do this?" They both looked at me in disbelief and tried not to laugh. They sheepishly began to teach me, "Well, you pull the cord here and then just kind of walk in straight lines until you're done." "Look, can you just show me?" I said with a confused look on my face. Daniel grabbed the lawn mower and began to push until I burst out laughing. They both then realized that I was joking, and we had a good laugh. I had developed a brotherhood with the men there, and we shared bonds that would never be broken. I still look back on my time there fondly and know that I wouldn't be where I am today if it wasn't for Christian Recovery Houses.

When I moved out, I found a little apartment on Wrightsville Beach about fifty feet from the sand. It was no mansion and had all sorts of critters living in it, but I loved it to death. My housemates around me were pretty wild, and we became friends quickly. It was yet another thing that made me realize how far I had come. During my last stint in recovery, I never would have been able to live in an environment with people who weren't in the same place as me—it would have been a danger to my sobriety. But now I encountered it as an opportunity to help others.

As time went on, I began to feel a tug on my heart. Deep down, I knew I would never attend law school. I knew that God had something different for me and that He was somehow going to use me in the context of the church. But I wasn't excited about it. The last thing I wanted to be was a part of what I saw as a problem. I didn't want to be the stereotypical pastor who people felt like they had to act differently around. I also thought I would struggle financially for the rest of my life if I decided to go that route. I had so many concerns about that line of work that I wouldn't allow myself to go down that path. But God wasn't worried. He always gets us where we are meant to be, regardless of what we may think about it.

11

POWER AND AUTHORITY

JAMES

*Come then thyself—to every heart the glory of thy
name make known; The means are our appointed
part, the power and grace are thine alone.*
JOHN NEWTON, *THE OLNEY HYMNS*

The metamorphosis God had brought about in Geoff's life was
beautiful. Even though I had prayed for it to happen for years,
it still caught us by surprise. Sure, I had believed God would
do something, but I didn't expect to see it for decades. *Maybe,
I thought, if I live to be eighty, he'll begin to come around and
I'll see some changes.* But this was so much better.

It was better because it happened regardless of my limited faith or the personal discouragement we faced on those days when it seemed like nothing would ever change. It was a reminder that God truly "is able to do immeasurably *more* than *all we ask or imagine*, according to his power that is at work within us" (Ephesians 3:20, emphasis added).

God's mercy goes so deep that we can never fully comprehend it. We find ourselves coming back and asking for reassurance, "Do you mean me? Is this for me and the ones I love?" And the answer is Yes! "Let anyone who is thirsty come to me and drink" (John 7:37). Even when the answer to our prayers for our loved ones is long in coming, or we do not see it for years (or at all during our lives on earth), God is still faithful to meet us and give us himself. We can keep coming to the Well of living water with our cracked and empty cups, and He will fill them again.

In the first couple of years after Geoffrey was set free, I found myself checking again and again to make sure a change had really occurred. When you're the parent of a former addict, you sometimes find yourself conditioned to think the worst. Even though you want to believe things are better, you find yourself hyper-vigilant, looking for any telltale sign that your child has fallen back into the pit he has just been pulled out of. You don't want to be that way, but you've been accustomed to an ongoing cycle for years. You go along thinking that all is well, and then . . . the relapse occurs. How could we know that the change with Geoffrey was lasting and real?

It took time, trust, and faith. Sometimes Geoff and I would have awkward conversations where I would tiptoe around the topic of relapse all too obviously. "What's the matter, Dad?" he asked on one occasion. "Don't you believe that Jesus has set me free?"

I didn't have a quick answer for that. It wasn't that I didn't have faith, but my faith (so I reasoned) was in God, not Geoff. My faith in Geoff was being rebuilt little by little. Still, I needed to ask whether my faith in God honestly allowed for the lasting change I was hoping for in Geoff. Could I trust God for that, after all we had been through? How much was up to Geoff, and how much was up to Him? In the struggle to sort things out, I found myself identifying with the father who came to Jesus and said: "Lord, I believe; help my unbelief!" (Mark 9:24 NKJV).

While God was restoring Geoffrey, He was also renewing our faith in His power to answer prayer. Through God's mercy, even the smallest amount of faith placed in Jesus's hands can work miracles. But here God was working on both of us yet again, challenging me to pray with new expectation and to look forward instead of backward—seeing Geoff not as he had been, but as the person God was making him to be.

As the months moved along, we increasingly discovered beautiful things in Geoff that evidenced the deeper work God was doing within. His recovery wasn't a fragile thing; it was vital and strong. We had never seen him so alive—he was being transformed from the inside out—his energy and even a childlike sense of wonder had been restored.

Meanwhile, God was using the hard things Geoff had been through to put new resolve and maturity into his character. He had new interests and new compassion for others and a wisdom that had been hard-won. God was even using the years he spent in addiction to help him get close to others who struggled in the same way and to make a difference in their lives for good.

Geoff was happy. He hadn't been this happy since his childhood. Life was an adventure again for him, and the trust between us was being rebuilt. Like the father in the parable of the prodigal, I had gotten my son back. And I felt like the party was just getting started.

Geoff headed back to school for the first time in years. Instead of flunking classes and being unable to finish as had happened in the past, he graduated from honors courses with an A average. He volunteered increasingly at Port City Church, helping with the Refuge substance abuse ministry and also serving elementary school-age children as a Sunday school volunteer. In addition, he was holding down a full-time job and doing well with it.

The change didn't happen all at once. Geoff grew into it over time, and his faith and resolve would be tested severely at times. Over the years that followed there would be trials and difficulties. A love relationship that ended in disappointment. A bad fall that resulted in a break in his wrist and caused him to be prescribed the same prescriptions he had once abused. But God brought him through all of it. Things that previously would have caused Geoff to relapse didn't.

Even through difficult seasons, he held on to His faith in God, and God never let him go—helping him make wiser choices and surrounding him with caring and believing friends. Geoff understood that even though he would struggle, his identity had been changed at the deepest level. He was no longer controlled or defined by a label or an addiction—he had become a child of God.

One day I had to laugh when we were talking and I made an off the cuff, overly flippant remark. Geoff looked at me and raised an eyebrow: "Did you run that by Jesus first?" he queried. It was a telling comment. He was learning to increasingly run more and more of his life by Jesus. The words that came out of his mouth, the music he listened to, the things that occupied his thoughts, and his time were increasingly being brought into the "glorious freedom" of the children of God (Romans 8:21 NLT).

Nowhere was this more evident than in worship. Sometimes we had the opportunity to join Geoff at a worship experience at the church or a Christian concert in the community. When Geoff was growing up, I had tried to point him to Christian worship music, but he had shown no interest. Now he embraced it from the heart without my prompting. Unbeknownst to Geoff (even at the time of this writing), I would frequently glance his way as he praised God—eyes closed, head raised, hands lifted up, giving himself in worship—and his actions in those moments spoke to me clearly of one who had been forgiven much and "loved much" as a result (Luke 7:47 NKJV). I found my own heart healing from wounds and fears of the past as I watched him there.

Geoff understood that he hadn't caused the change in his life; he had let the change in. It was work to do that, but the deeper and abiding work was God's. One day, just short of two years into his new freedom in Christ, the family gathered for Thanksgiving. Ever cautious, while I understood that Geoff was doing well, I wanted him to stay on his guard against the difficulties the devil throws our way. So I pulled him away from the family for a few minutes just to talk. We drove a couple of miles to the gas station and while we were waiting for our tank to fill I asked him about several areas of his life, wanting to make sure he was still okay. "Remember, Son" I told him, "we have an adversary, and he is powerful." Geoff looked me in the eye and didn't miss a beat: "I know, Dad. He has power. But he has no authority."

I'll remember those words as long as I live, and then some. Jesus said, "All authority has been given to *Me* in heaven and on earth" (Matthew 28:18 NKJV, emphasis added). Through His authority, my son had been restored to me. "He was lost and is found" (Luke 15:24). And I will be thanking God for that for eternity.

GEOFF

A safe fairyland is untrue to all worlds.
J. R. R. TOLKIEN, *THE LETTERS OF J. R. R. TOLKIEN*

"I have some free time if you need help around the church!" I told Brett as we cleaned up after Tsunami one night. I was entering my last semester earning my associate's degree, and I only had two classes—leaving me with plenty of free time. "Yeah, man, that would be awesome. We actually just had an intern leave and would love to have you fill in." Brett happily accepted my offer and put me to work. There was always something to do and extra help was rarely turned down.

Over the next few months I did everything from picking up chairs to communicating on stage, and I grew to love it. The more time I spent with students, the more I was reminded of a time in my life that I missed. My own personal season of being an innocent middle school student who didn't have a care in the world other than pizza and video games was decidedly short. Middle school is a formative time for students. It is often the time when you begin to own your faith or when you decide to go the other way. I enjoyed being there to push students toward Jesus, and I considered it a proactive fight against addiction.

At the same time, I was still volunteering my time in Refuge. Mark invested in me and showed me the ropes of ministry. I learned how to speak before large groups, how to care for people pastorally, and how to be there when everything was falling apart. As my time in school began to draw to a close, God had finally turned my heart. I knew I was being called into ministry and that if I tried to do anything else I would never be satisfied. It was hard to turn away from one kind of success attainable through spending several more years in school, but I knew God had a different story for me.

For the longest time, I waited for a job I was interested in to open up at PC3. I probably would have done anything, but there was really no opportunity in sight. I thought about going back to school to finish my degree, but that would involve leaving town and going somewhere else or attending online. If I was going to continue my education, it would be with a ministry focus.

When something did finally open up at the church, I was ecstatic and thought it was the perfect job for me. I quickly turned in my resume, but I didn't even get an interview. I was frustrated and hurt because I had already convinced myself I was going to get the position. I thought I would have loved it, but as time went on, I saw that God had something better.

A few months later, the director of the high school ministry (Ripple Effect) decided to move on, and some restructuring took place at the church. The church moved Brett to director over both middle school and high school and opened up three available positions: High School Coordinator, Middle School Coordinator, and Middle School Volunteer Coordinator. Those main coordinators were essentially pastoral positions. They directed the entire ministry, were the main teachers, planned events, and cared for students. I thought the church would want someone with a lot of experience in those roles, but I was excited about the volunteer coordinator role that had opened, albeit part-time.

I reached out to one of the pastors at the church and asked him about the position. He took me out to breakfast and after I had shown interest in the part-time job, he encouraged me to apply for one of the full-time positions. I was surprised. I felt unqualified and unsure if I was ready for so much responsibility in a ministry context. This was different from anything I had expected, and at times my previous life didn't feel so far away. I always thought that I would work with people in addictions—never students—but I moved forward in faith, regardless. As I continued to pray about it, God made it clear that I was in the right place. After a flurry of interviews, much to my surprise, I was hired as the High School Coordinator.

Following that, life became near perfect. My relationship with my family had improved greatly, and it had been four years since I had used heroin. People who heard my story hardly believed where I had come from. I was in a romantic relationship that I was sure would last forever, and I began to put down roots in Wilmington. I had what felt like a fairytale story that everyone loved to hear, and I blissfully floated through life for quite a while.

At times, it seemed like things were too good, and I would find myself waiting for everything to come crashing down.

Unfortunately, I wasn't waiting in vain. The next year of my life was the most difficult I have ever lived through. It wasn't as dramatic as my life in addiction and didn't involve crime or a crazy lifestyle. This time the pain was different. My relationship that seemed so bright had unexpectedly fallen apart, and it felt like everyone was watching it happen. At the same time, I was coming to terms with the difficult side of working in ministry and learning how to handle the pressure. Moreover, I also lost the majority of my savings on real estate I had purchased. Back-to-back, I suffered devastating blows to my life and the things that I had put so much earthly stock in.

For the first time in a long time, my circumstances had become bleak. It wasn't the same things I had been through in the past, and I was learning to cope with pain differently. When I was in my addiction, I could numb myself to the outside world, and things didn't faze me because I couldn't feel. I had little to no emotions and if I began to feel some, I would quickly kill them with another high. No longer could I mask the pain; it was time to learn to deal with it.

Another aspect that made these situations difficult is that in all of them I had little to no control. There was nothing I could do about my circumstances, and at times I felt completely helpless and angry. I had lost the perspective I had before, and I felt entitled to the things I had earned. I reasoned with God that after everything I had been through I shouldn't have to go through more. But over time He would reveal what I needed to see.

I don't know that I would have made it through that season of life without my friends and coworkers who were there for me. I often pushed them away or told them that I was fine, but they continually returned with grace, love, and kindness. It was yet another display of God's wisdom and mercy through my community of faith.

My hobbies were also important aspects of working through those times. Surfing, skating, and spearfishing were places of comfort for me when I was struggling. I always knew that when life got overwhelming, I could go hang out in the ocean or at the skatepark. In God's perfect timing, I was given a dog, a wild labradoodle named Rosie, who became one of my best friends in that dark time. Her endless joy and unconditional love were always present.

I got in the habit of allowing Rosie to pull me around my neighborhood on a skateboard. It helped get her energy out and we both loved it, so we did it every day. One Sunday morning as we were flying around my street, I turned to wave to a neighbor who was outside. As I did, Rosie steered me over a manhole cover. My skateboard hit it, caught, and threw me into the pavement. I felt my arm break instantaneously, and I tried to get up. When I did, my arm fell to a crooked angle. I knew if I tried to move, it would be worse. My neighbor helped construct a makeshift splint out of a cereal box and I called my friend, Sarah, who lived down the street, to come pick me up.

On arrival at the hospital, I was immediately given a dose of opiates to help with the pain. They then put me under, reset my bone, and scheduled me for surgery. After my surgery, I was prescribed opiates to get me through the healing process. I had seen friends in recovery go through this before, and there were typically two strategies. One, out of both wisdom and fear, a person took no medications and dealt with the pain. Or two, a person took them with a lot of accountability. I didn't want to make my decision out of fear, so I decided to have Sarah hold onto my prescription and give them to me as needed. It was strange to feel the effects of opiates again, albeit legally this time. My life of addiction had been far away up to that point, but now the primary offender was right back in my face.

At first, I felt confident and thought I was safe. As time went on, though, the enemy was probing for any weakness. Things were already difficult because of my recent circumstances, and being back on opiates brought me to a potentially dark place. I struggled with depression. I had stitches that ran from my elbow to my wrist, along with a new addition of a large plate with nearly a dozen screws. Once my prescription was nearing an end, I began to realize the danger I was in. Gradually my relationship with God had begun to take a back seat. Old emotions started to creep in, and I began to be easily frustrated.

At that point, I knew it was time to expose things to the light and make them visible (Ephesians 5:13). God had allowed my faith to be tested in this time, but He also gave me the courage to go to others in the church and confide in them about my recent struggles. He exposed the frustration and the fragile place I had ended up in. He also exposed an encroaching sense of pride and entitlement.

Once those things were brought into the light, just as God promises, He was "faithful and just" to forgive me (1 John 1:9), and He continued to give me every support I needed. I am continually reminded of God's love and mercy by the people around me, and I don't know what life would look like without them. The beautiful thing about that dark season was that it returned me to a desperate reliance on God and renewed my love for Him.

It can be easy to make our walk with God a cool sideshow to the main attraction of work, family, or things that we prioritize before Him. We praise Him for the things we like and turn inward for the things we don't. We go to Him when we need something and are quick to walk away as soon as we receive it. I had nearly forgotten that the new life and identity I received was given to me by God and God alone. I almost lost my grasp on the truth that I remained hopelessly in need of His grace and guidance.

I share this because I realize that whenever my family and I tell our story, there is always someone in the room who feels cynical and isolated. For every person who thanks us and gives us hugs because of how we were able to help, there is another person who is frustrated and hurting because our story was not theirs. That person is the reason I feel it is important to share this part of my story. I do not want to paint the picture that life is perfect with Jesus and that nothing ever goes wrong. Some things about it are more difficult than ever before, and tough things still happen. Things come to pass that we wish never did. Life is rarely rainbows and sunshine, and when it is, it doesn't always last long.

But there is beauty even in the ups and downs. Christ came to give us life—life to the full (John 10:10). Part of that fullness of life is experiencing a full range of emotions. The good, the bad, the ugly are all a part of living a full life, and we get to do it under the refuge of His wings (Psalm 91:4). The truth is that while I went through a difficult and refining season, God was still faithful.

I used to blame God for my addiction, thinking that He caused it to happen so I would be able to use my story to help others. When bad things would happen to people, I would give God the responsibility for it and then look for the good things that came out of it.

Over time, I have come to realize how wise our God is. He doesn't cause terrible things to happen so He can use them for good. Rather, we are people with free will. We do things that God would never have us do, and in turn, terrible things come to pass. Then God, in His beautiful mercy, takes these terrible things and works them for our good (Romans 8:28).

Isn't it just like our God? Just like the cross? To take an ugly, horrible, unredeemable tool of torture and turn it into a symbol of freedom and love. God did it then and He still does it . . . countless times every single day. He has forever given us hope in the darkest of times, hope that holds on to us, and He will always prevail.

12

Overtaken by Love

James

Quarry me deep, dear Lord, and then fill me
to overflowing with living water.
A Puritan Prayer, *The Valley of Vision*

Today Geoff is a youth pastor in the same city where he once abused heroin. He serves hundreds of kids each week with the goal of pointing them to the hope he has found in Jesus Christ and helping them avoid making the mistakes he made. It is valuable, soul-shaping work of eternal worth.

We also frequently travel and speak together, sharing the change God has brought about in his life. I am amazed at how we got here. God mercifully brought us through each twist and turn, making a way through the wasteland. When I first asked Geoffrey if it was okay if I shared our story and the transformation God had made in his life, I wanted to be careful not to disclose too much. But his response caught me off guard: "Dad, I want you to tell it. I prefer that you tell my story, because it's pointless if others don't hear it. Why else would God have done it?"

Redemption is a breathtaking thing. Geoff is a better man today because of the mistakes he's made. God used them to forge new strengths in his character and to give us both a deep assurance of His power to save us and set us free—regardless of human wisdom about the odds against us. Do we both wish he had made other choices earlier in life? Absolutely. But if he had, we would not have seen God's mercy as "the One who breaks open the way" (Micah 2:13) and rescues us from every captivity. Our aim in writing this book has been to share our story in a way that is brutally honest about our own shortcomings, making clear that God alone got us through.

As I am writing these words, someone dies every eleven minutes because of the opioid crisis in the United States.[10] One day, after Geoff and I finished speaking at a church in New England, a father who had lost his son and had four other children addicted to heroin approached me. "We've been through what you've experienced five times over and more," he said bitterly. It would be an understatement to say my heart went out to him.

Why didn't God answer his prayers in the same way as ours? Why have other parents had to see their worst fears realized with their prodigals when they prayed and fasted and believed things would be better? Only God knows the answer.

We have been spared much. So many parents who have prayed faithfully for years (longer than we) have not seen a change for good in their prodigals' lives. Others—like family members very close to us—have seen their addicted child place his faith in Jesus and later relapse and go to be with Him forever. Still others have prayed and seen immediate change, and transformation every bit as beautiful as we have witnessed in Geoff.

How does one process these things? A cynical person might say that our prayers don't make any difference, that we're just speaking words into the air and what we regard as answers are merely self-persuasion. But the witness of God's Word affirms that our prayers matter more than we know.

There are mysteries here. There are times when we may feel abandoned by God although He is actually very close. Our circumstances overwhelm us, and perhaps we cannot sense His presence. I recently heard an overseas missionary, who had been imprisoned and persecuted for two years for his faith, describe how one day he was lamenting before God that he felt deserted by Him. But as he continued to pray and pour his heart out to God, the words that came out of his mouth surprised him. He found himself saying, "I love you, Lord Jesus." And that surprised him. Even if he didn't have the answers for why God seemed distant, God's love was still present, sustaining him on a level that was deeper than he knew, deeper even than his emotions.

It was in the very middle of his lament that Jeremiah discovered, "Because of the LORD's great love we are not consumed, for his compassions never fail. They are new every morning; great is your faithfulness" (Lamentations 3:22–23).

One of the lasting lessons of our journey with Geoff has been a hard-won understanding that prayer is about so much more than our requests and answers. We were driven to pray because we were desperately seeking solutions, but along the way we discovered that something else was happening. Many times when I went to God in the fever of the moment wanting to see something done, His response seemed to be, "As long as you're here talking with me about Geoff, why don't you stay and rest awhile? While you are waiting, let's spend a moment together. Just be with Me, and I will restore your soul."

When nothing seemed to change in our immediate circumstances or even got worse, God still had ways of showing himself faithful. He was teaching us that the purpose of prayer isn't first about asking and receiving, it's about keeping company with Him. God himself is the best answer to prayer when answers don't seem to come. We would not have experienced His peace—how God met us and carried us through the darkest days—had we not been driven to pray. The cry of our hearts for our son laid bare our need, but our need went deeper still.

Helmut Thielicke wrote, "The greatest mysteries of God are always enacted in the depths; and therefore it is the cry from the depths that always has the greatest promise."[11] We needed to discover how to lean into Him in the moment so that we might live in the truth that David discovered: "The LORD is my shepherd, I lack nothing" (Psalm 23:1).

This growing discovery of the depth and reliability of God's love has been the greatest blessing of our journey, and it was made before Geoff was set free from his addiction. That matters, because God is more than the measure of things that happen to us for good or ill. Comfort comes as we wait *with* Jesus. If we wait *for* Him, our eyes are continually on our circumstances, and we will find little strength there. But if we wait *with* Him in our longing for our loved ones to turn to Him, and turn our worries into prayer, He will show us that He is more than enough. He will get us through each day, and beyond. "Neither death nor life, neither angels nor demons, neither the present nor the future, nor any powers, neither height nor depth, nor anything else in all creation, will be able to separate us from the love of God that is in Christ Jesus our Lord" (Romans 8:38–39).

We cannot see all that God is doing in answer to our prayers in a given moment. William Cowper's words are on point here: "Blind unbelief is sure to err and scan His work in vain; God is His own interpreter, and He will make it plain." It's heartbreaking when we see the life of someone we love dearly shatter in a thousand broken pieces, but even those shards may be wisely, carefully, lovingly put together into a mosaic of unsurpassed beauty when placed in God's hands through prayer.

Halfway through the writing of this book, I narrated the audiobook version of *Prayers for Prodigals* at the Our Daily Bread Ministries studio in Grand Rapids, Michigan. It was completed in two days, but it could have taken one. As I read aloud through the book, I had to keep stopping because my voice kept breaking. At the time *Prayers for Prodigals* was written, it was a book of unanswered prayers for my son. But eight years later there were so many prayers I had forgotten I had prayed—so many cries from the heart that had eventually been answered in God's own time and way—I was overcome by emotion as I read through them.

Those two days became a poignant lesson in God's wisdom and timing. I had prayed for Geoff's freedom from substance abuse, for God to keep my son when he was far away, for trust between us to be restored, for Geoff to return from the far country and to discover "how wide and long and high and deep is the love of Christ" (Ephesians 3:18). There are still prayers in the book that have yet to be answered. I have another dear one I've been praying for longer than Geoff, but God's kindness to him gives me hope that we will see another prayer answered. And as long as we have Him to look forward to, hope not only lies ahead but it can also meet us anytime, anywhere.

Not long ago, I ran into Mr. Lock, one of Geoffrey's former high school principals, in a local warehouse store. When I used to encounter him years ago, I would keep the conversation brief to avoid the inevitable question, "How's Geoff doing these days?" This time I steered my cart in his direction. As I shared the details about Geoff's new life—what Jesus had saved him from, the man he has become, his work as a youth pastor giving back to God and others—a thoughtful smile came to Mr. Lock's face.

"One thing I've learned in my line of work," he said, "is never freeze a kid in time. Geoff's story is beautiful."

As I walked away, my mind went back to the uncomfortable conversations Mr. Lock and I had about my son many years ago in his office, and as I got to the parking lot, I found myself in awe yet again of what God had done.

Geoff's story *is* beautiful. God truly rescued him. He redeemed him and rebuilt him and sent him to serve. And other lives have been transformed because of it, including our own. We never saw that coming.

In Psalm 23 the words "Surely your goodness and love will *follow* me all the days of my life" (v. 6, emphasis added) contain a meaning that is often overlooked. The Hebrew word for follow in that verse is an active word that can also be translated "pursue." We have been pursued by God's unrelenting goodness and kindness, and we were overtaken just when it seemed like things were at their worst.

When God pursues you with inexhaustible love, it is a very good thing to be caught.

GEOFF

Please, Lord. Let me get one more.
DESMOND DOSS, *HACKSAW RIDGE*

I have been grateful to call Wilmington, North Carolina, my home again for several years. It is the most beautiful place I have ever lived, and many good people live here. Unfortunately, that beauty is being countered by a terrible epidemic. According to a 2016 study by Castlight Health, a California-based healthcare information company, Wilmington was the number one city in the US per capita for opioid abuse. This is evident when you walk around certain areas of the city and see needles and other paraphernalia littering the street. There are frequent reports of large drug busts on the news, and other issues of violence and theft are commonplace.

While Castlight's report certainly brought us a bad name, it also opened a lot of people's eyes to what is happening not just in Wilmington but all over the US. People are now paying attention, striving to make a difference in the opiate crisis in our cities. I have sat in room after room full of people of all ages who have been affected by addiction.

One evening after a recovery event at a church in Plymouth, Massachusetts, a little girl who must have been about five years old came up to me. Her mother said she had a question for me, so I knelt down to get on her level and look her in the eyes. "What's your question, little one?" I laughed, expecting a light-hearted response. She looked me in the eyes and quietly mumbled, "Why did my daddy have to die doing bad things, but you didn't?"

I was speechless. I knew I would never understand what this little girl was going through, but I did my best to respond: "Sometimes things happen that aren't fair. It's okay to be angry, to be hurt, to feel however you are feeling, and I trust that someday God is going to use your story to help people," I told her, with tears welling up in my eyes. I hurt so badly for that little girl. I could understand her thinking that it really wasn't fair. I had thought that many times myself, long before she asked me. Why did I make it through my addiction, but so many fathers, mothers, sons, daughters, brothers, and sisters do not? Why me?

I do not know the answer to that question. But I do know what I can do in response: I can try to be a part of making a difference. I have been so encouraged to see the church step into these issues the way it has in recent years. Many Christian organizations have partnered with schools, the government, and even law enforcement to provide aid to people in addiction. The church we visited that night in New England was holding that kind of event.

The church I serve (Port City Community Church) was able to host an incredible event called MVMT (Movement) where all the community organizations and resources that helped with substance abuse, regardless of their varying perspectives, came together to make a difference. It has opened avenues of communication between people who were previously separated. That is important, because community matters immensely. People loving each other, helping each other, and being there for each other are the things it will take to crush addiction.

Please know that if you have a loved one who is in this, you do not have to be alone. Neither do they. There's a growing number of us who have walked this road and who have discovered God's mercy along the way.

When I think back on my story, there are many things I will never forget and feelings I will never be able to shake.

- Detoxing on the floor of that jail.
- Talking to my family through a plexiglass wall with a jumpsuit on.
- Sitting in the courtroom.
- Lying in the hospital bed after my wreck.

In all of those moments, I felt utterly alone and helpless. I thought no one understood, no one could help, and no one would be there when it was over. But through all of that, God hadn't abandoned me.

So, alongside of those moments, other things—good things—I will never forget stand in contrast.

- My parents continually being there for me no matter what.

- The nurse not allowing me to leave that treatment center, even at risk to her job.
- Eric, my counselor, pulling me aside to encourage me.
- The people who loved me at church regardless of how I acted.
- Others who took a chance on me and invested in my life when the only reason they had for doing so was God.

When I think of those moments and so many others, I feel loved, cared for, and valued. Not because of anything I have done—but only because of the goodness of God. It was this love that brought me to Jesus and allowed me to change. It's the Lord's kindness that leads to repentance (Romans 2:4), and He shows us that kindness through His people.

Today, I spend most of my days hanging out with high school students. I am constantly reminded of who I was when I was their age, and I love watching their wheels turn as they ask the same questions I asked back then. I love helping them wrestle through what it is like to walk with God and to learn how to be there for people. It is an incredible, beautiful gift that someone like me has been able to experience the redemption Jesus gives and now has the opportunity to share it.

My family and I have continued to strengthen and rebuild our relationships over the years, and I'm grateful for that. Looking back, I realize there were so many times I should have died, so many times I shouldn't have awakened.

But I did.

Sometimes, the only difference I see between me and many of my friends who didn't make it is the fact that I had praying parents at home who never gave up on me. Even when I disappointed them, lied to them, and stole from them—they never abandoned me. Parents who pray for their prodigals give them an amazing gift, and they receive new strength themselves.

Not long ago, a popular Christian TV show came and recorded my story, and they brought my father and me on. It was broadcast all over the world, and a lot of people were exposed to our story because of it. Many have reached out to me since then, but none of them have surprised me like an old friend who got in touch soon afterwards.

My phone sent me a notification, and I picked it up to see a message on Facebook Messenger. It was an old partner I used to sell drugs with years ago. I was unsure what the message was going to be about, but when I opened it, it read, "Hey man, I was flipping through TV the other night and saw your face on the screen so I stopped. I watched your entire story and listened to you talk. It was so encouraging to see how much you've changed. I have been struggling with pills still, and your story made me decide to go to rehab. Thank you for that. And keep your head up, because you never know who is watching."

I was floored. This was the same guy who used to sling all sorts of drugs with me back in the day. He was hard, and people were afraid to mess with him. I hadn't talked to him in years and to get that message from him at the time was eye-opening.

We never know what God is up to. His resourcefulness and creativity are amazing. He is constantly working for our good, tying all sorts of loose ends together. Often, I find that when it feels as if He is doing nothing, He is actually diligently at work at a level deeper than I thought.

We don't serve a weak, powerless, or inattentive God. We serve the God who created the universe and called into existence our very beings. He is infinite in both His love and His wisdom.

Sometimes things don't look like we think they should. For years, my family watched me try to get by without God. Then, when Christ prevailed in my heart, it took a long time for the evidence to show. My life didn't look like it should have, but God never gave up on me either.

Not only was He at work in my heart but also in my parents' hearts as well. We all were learning to trust God in deeper ways, and He used our difficult circumstances to do that. My friend Dermot always says that "Addiction is a family disease. You can measure the severity of it not by how much you use, but by how many relationships you destroy." I know that sentiment rings true for many people as they walk through this with a loved one, but fortunately, there is hope. We serve a relational God. We can see His power through the things He rebuilds, the relationships He reconciles, and the way He loves.

A relationship with Jesus is a journey. It is not an easy one or a short one. Things will happen that will shake you to your core and make you wonder if He is even there. I constantly remind myself today that I have to trust. I have to trust God with my relationships. I have to trust Him with my circumstances. I have to trust Him with my life. He is active, moving, and present even when we can't tell.

I frequently return to the verse that I stumbled on that evening when I was detoxing in the treatment center:

When you pass through the waters, I will be with you;
and when you pass through the rivers, they will not
sweep over you.
When you walk through the fire, you will not be burned;
the flames will not set you ablaze. (Isaiah 43:2)

There will be floods and fires, there will be difficulties and hardships, but in those same moments, there will also be God.

That "life verse" for me is now accompanied by another:

Therefore be imitators of God, as beloved children.
(Ephesians 5:1 ESV)

I'm not who I once was. I am a child of God now. He has given me identity and purpose. I am to love like Him, forgive like Him, serve like Him.

I have been set free.

ACKNOWLEDGMENTS

JAMES

This has been a challenging book to work on. We had to recall moments and years, sins and mistakes we might have wanted to forget (but I'm glad that we didn't). I want to thank Geoff for his bravery in taking the risk of telling our story. Your candor in sharing your past is already an encouragement to many, reflecting the one, true Light of the World (John 8:12) to those who are still in dark and desperate places. I couldn't be more proud of you, Son.

I also would like to express profound gratitude to the team at Our Daily Bread Publishing, including the many behind the scenes who have contributed in significant ways. Miranda Gardner and Ken Petersen, your thoughtful support for this atypical endeavor speaks of your breadth of spirit and heart to serve others. Dawn Anderson, you received the baton from Miranda mid-race and have run beautifully (in your own shoes!). Dave Branon, your gentleness in handling our story, your skillful work and God-given insights have once again made for a better book—to say I thank God for you doesn't go far enough. But He knows what words cannot express.

So many others have had a hand not just in this book, but in our lives: Ken Davis, Bruce and Jan Gray, Lynn Wiemann, Bob and Pam Dodson, Mike Ashcraft, Keith Cobb, Margaret Shockley, Shirilee Little—what a blessing you are! Mark Allen, Daniel Summers, Elizabeth Mixon, Gary Sauls, Roxanne Ellington, your friendship to our family in the most challenging of times has truly been a gift from God. When others may not have understood, you have—and the years continue to show the difference you have made.

Caridad, your indefatigable love and compassion have made our story complete. You are aptly named "Charity," and it is a joy to walk through life with you. Stefani, your love for your brother has always made me smile.

The last and greatest thank you belongs to You, our Savior and our strength. Every praise is yours, and ever will be. Above every hope and expectation, you are "The One who breaks open the way" (Micah 2:13), and you make "everything new" (Revelation 21:5). Soli Deo Gloria.

GEOFF

As my father said, this book was a challenge to write. Some of the wounds that we had to examine in the process turned out to still be open, but there was so much healing along the way. I could not be more grateful for my parents, James and Cari, and my sister, Stefani. Our family has been through so much together, and the love that we have because of it is something that I will never take for granted.

The story that we were able to tell never would have happened if it weren't for so many people in my community. Mark Allen,

Daniel and Jennifer Summers, Mike Ashcraft, Elizabeth Mixon, Hunter Scanlan, Chris Sasser, Dermot Gibney, Sonny Russel, the Pigfords, Brett Eddy—the list could go on and on. Thank you for being there for me in the darkest of times and encouraging me the whole way. I count all of you among family and love each of you dearly.

Sarah, thank you for encouraging me and loving me even when my schedule was full and I slept very little. You picked me up when no one else could, and I am so grateful for who you are. I love you so much and am so excited to be a part of your life moving forward.

There are people who were a part of my story when I was still addicted that I hurt. Ashley, Kate, Sandy, Mike, and many others. Some of you I have reconciled with, others I haven't, but regardless, I apologize for the wounds I caused and hope that you can forgive me for the person I was. I pray that God blesses all of you for the trouble I caused in your life.

There are so many people I wish I could thank individually that have been a part of my life, but I would end up writing another book. So, to those of you who have encouraged me along the way, thank you.

This story represents a community of people who are trying to better themselves and change the world for the better. Whether you are still addicted, in recovery, or somewhere in between, know that there is always hope.

Lastly, thank you to Port City Community Church and Peace Church for supporting me and believing in me, even when no one else would. You are a beautiful picture of the love of Christ.

Appendix A

Excerpts from *Prayers for Prodigals*

For Freedom from Substance Abuse

Be careful, or your hearts will be weighed down with
carousing, drunkenness and the anxieties of life.
LUKE 21:34

He's not being careful, Lord.
His heart is "weighed down with carousing, drunkenness
and the anxieties of life," and he doesn't even know it.
He's given in to the world's message that he's "having
a good time," but he isn't.
He's complicated his life in ways that hurt to see.

"Who has woe? Who has sorrow? Who has strife? Who has complaints?

Who has needless bruises? Who has bloodshot eyes?

Those who linger over wine" (Proverbs 23:29–30).

There's been too much lingering, Lord. He likes it too much.

And "in the end it bites like a snake and poisons like a viper" (Proverbs 23:32).

But I praise you, Father. You are the one who says "to the captives, 'Come out,' and to those in darkness, 'Be free!'" (Isaiah 49:9).

Call him out, Lord! Out of darkness, out of carousing, out of any

substance or drug abuse, and out of relationships that contribute to these things.

I can see him set free, Lord. Shining from head to foot, smiling and strong, a living example of your kindness and love.

He has "spent enough time in the past doing what pagans choose to do" (1 Peter 4:3).

Set him free, Father!

I know that he has to want to be free. So I ask you to open his eyes to see the consequences of his actions, and let him long for something more.

Let him "hunger and thirst for righteousness," for then he "will be filled" and blessed (Matthew 5:6)!

Let him "be filled with the Spirit" (Ephesians 5:18), because "where the Spirit of the Lord is, there is freedom" (2 Corinthians 3:17).

Lord Jesus, you came "to proclaim freedom for the captives and release from darkness for the prisoners" (Isaiah 61:1).

Help my son, Lord—he's a prisoner of his addictions.

I pray that he be "brought into the glorious freedom of the children of God" in every way (Romans 8:21)!

I thank you that you are completely able to do this, Father.

You are able to keep him "from falling and to present" him before your "glorious presence without fault and with great joy" (Jude 1:24).

Let your joy be so real to him that he won't seek happiness in anything less.

I praise you in advance for the day he will tell you, "You have filled my heart with greater joy" (Psalm 4:7).

Let that day be today!

FOR THE KEEPING OF ANGELS

See that you do not despise one of these little ones. For I tell you that their angels in heaven always see the face of my Father in heaven.
MATTHEW 18:10

Your Word says you send your angels to do your "bidding," Father (Psalm 103:20).

Thank you for giving our children angels who "always see" your face.

Thank you for all the times you've looked after my child when I could not: the near misses, the fraction-of-a-second, happened-too-fast-for-me-to-react moments when your angel intervened.

My child needs the protection of your angels now, Lord.

Just like when you sent one to watch over Daniel and "shut the mouths of the lions" (Daniel 6:22).

I need your angels to go where I cannot go, just as you did the nights you rescued Peter "from Herod's clutches" (Acts 12:11) and "opened the doors of the jail" for the apostles (Acts 5:19).

I know some might think it presumptuous of me to ask for angels for someone who is not where he's supposed to be, but you've done this before.

You did it for Elijah when he "was afraid and ran for his life" (1 Kings 19:3). "All at once an angel touched him" twice (1 Kings 19:5, 7).

You also had your angels take Lot's hand "when he hesitated" to leave Sodom with his family, because you were "merciful to them" (Genesis 19:16).

You are merciful, Lord! And you said that "whatever you loose on earth will be loosed in heaven" (Matthew 18:18).

So I ask that you send an angel from heaven to help my son.

Just as "some people have entertained angels without knowing it" (Hebrews 13:2), let a stranger show him a kindness that he knows is from you.

Or, as when you sent your angels to shepherds with the "good news" of Jesus (Luke 2:10), send someone to share your love and your presence with him so that he will believe, seek you out, and bow before you.

You've said that "the angel of the Lord encamps around those who fear him, and he delivers them" (Psalm 34:7).

Because I "know what it is to fear" you (2 Corinthians 5:11), Lord, with reverence, awe, and love, I ask that you deliver my son.

Your Word tells me about what you've done for those you call your own: "In all their distress he too was distressed, and the angel of his presence saved them. In his love and mercy he redeemed them" (Isaiah 63:9).

Redeem my son, Lord! Let him be a joy to you and to all of heaven, because "there is rejoicing in the presence of the angels of God over one sinner who repents" (Luke 15:10).

I don't know how you will do it, but I ask you to help him open his heart to you.

I'd love to know how you're going to do it, Lord, but I know that "even angels long to look into these things" (1 Peter 1:12).

So I will watch and pray and wait, and say with the angels, "Praise and glory and wisdom and thanks and honor and power and strength be to our God for ever and ever. Amen!" (Revelation 7:11–12).

Appendix B

RESOURCES

WEBSITE

Encouraging Prayer at JamesBanks.org. Parents may enter anonymous requests for their children on the "Prodigal Prayer Wall" at this site. Please also visit the "Prayer Resources" page and click on the "Praying for Prodigals" tab for additional resources and video interviews with James and Geoff.

BOOKS

On Prayer and Parenting
Banks, James. *Prayers for Prodigals*. Grand Rapids, MI: Discovery House, 2011.
————. *Prayers for Your Children*. Grand Rapids, MI: Discovery House, 2015.

————. *Praying the Prayers of the Bible for Everyday Needs*. Grand Rapids, MI: Discovery House, 2018.

Bell Graham, Ruth. *Prodigals (and Those Who Love Them)*. Grand Rapids, MI: Baker Books, 2008.

Morgan, Robert J. *Moments for Families with Prodigals*. Colorado Springs, CO: NavPress, 2003.

Biographies and Autobiographies

Cymbala Toledo, Chrissy. *The Girl in the Song*. Carol Stream, IL: Tyndale Momentum, 2015.

Graham, Franklin. *Rebel with a Cause*. Nashville, TN: Thomas Nelson, 1995.

Miller, John, and Barbara Miller Juliani. *Come Back, Barbara*. Phillipsburg, NJ: P & R Publishing, 1997.

Yuan, Christopher, and Angela Yuan. *Out of a Far Country*: A Gay Son's Journey to God. Colorado Springs, CO: WaterBrook Press, 2011.

Related to Recovery and Addiction

Berenson, Alex. *Tell Your Children: The Truth about Marijuana, Mental Illness, and Violence*, New York, NY: Free Press, 2019.

Butterfield, Rosia Champagne. *The Secret Thoughts of an Unlikely Convert*. Pittsburgh, PA: Crown & Covenant, 2012.

Welch, Edward T. *Addictions: A Banquet in the Grave*. Phillipsburg, NJ: P & R Publishing, 2001.

Wilkerson, Mike. *Redemption*. Wheaton, IL: Crossway Books, 2011.

Yuan, Christopher. *Holy Sexuality and the Gospel*. Colorado Springs, CO: Multnomah Books, 2018.

Notes

1. James Banks, *Prayers for Prodigals* (Grand Rapids, MI: Discovery House, 2011), 67.
2. C. S. Lewis, *Mere Christianity* (Westwood, NJ: Barbour, 1952), 107.
3. Cited in Alex Berenson, *Tell Your Children* (New York: Free Press, 2019), xxx.
4. Charles Spurgeon, "The Master Key—Opening the Gate of Heaven," *The C. H. Spurgeon Collection*, vol. 33, https://www.spurgeongems.org/vols31-33/chs1938.pdf.
5. James Banks, *Prayers for Prodigals* (Grand Rapids, MI: Discovery House, 2011), 38–39.
6. T. S. Eliot, "The Hollow Men" *The Complete Poems and Plays: 1909–1950* (New York: Harcourt Brace, 1980).
7. Ole Hallesby, *Prayer* (Minneapolis, MN: Augsburg Fortress, 1994), 18.
8. Jim Cymbala, *Fresh Wind, Fresh Fire* (Grand Rapids, MI: Zondervan, 1997), 60–66.
9. Peter Taylor Forsyth, *The Soul of Prayer* (Seaside, OR: 1916 Edition republished by Rough Draft Printing, 2012), 65.

10. Shreeya Sinha and Jennifer Harlan, "Heroin Addiction Explained: How Opioids Hijack the Brain," nytimes.com/interactive/2018/8s/addition-heroin-opioids.html (September 24, 2019).
11. Helmut Thielicke, *Our Heavenly Father* (New York: Harper and Brothers, 1953), 64.